Bossing Up

BOSSING UP PUBLICATIONS

BOSSING UP. Copyright © 2017 by Samantha Kris. All rights reserved. No part of this book may be used or reproduced in any manner whatsoever without written permission except in the case of brief quotations in the context of critical articles or reviews.

For information: Samantha@samanthakris.com

Book design: Lorena Rossi, Grind Atelier

Developmental edits: Alexa Nazzaro, Aaxel Author Services

Illustrations: Leigh Jeffery, Comix Central

Back cover photo: Karolina Jez

ISBN 978-1-7750244-0-8

Dedication

For all the Bosses who are simultaneously a masterpiece and a work in progress

SUCCESS

- HAPPINESS
- ACCEPTANCE
- CONFIDENCE
- BALANCE
- GROWTH
- FORGIVENESS
- MONEY
- GOALS

Table of Contents

Dedication iii

Bossing Up Defined ix

Prelude 1

My Bossing Up Journey 3

Success Stoppers 13

Part 1: Know What You Want 17

    Chapter 1: I'm All Ears 23

    Chapter 2: The Woman in the Mirror 31

    Chapter 3: Car Crashes, Canyons, and Sharks 41

    Chapter 4: What You Weren't Taught in School 51

Part 2: Avoid Pursuing Imposed Success 59

    Chapter 5: Life's Greatest Challenge 65

    Chapter 6: Ctrl Alt Del 73

    Chapter 7: There's Been a Change of Plans 79

    Chapter 8: Nah 87

Part 3: Focus on Progress Instead of Perfection 95

    Chapter 9: Words Not to Live By 101

    Chapter 10: ~~Tomorrow~~ 111

    Chapter 11: Usain Walked Before Usain Bolt 117

    Chapter 12: Wing It 123

    Chapter 13: You Can't Multitask 131

    Chapter 14: Treat Yo'self 141

Chapter 15: Doors Are for Opening 149

Chapter 16: So, You're a Hot Mess 157

Chapter 17: Why Are You Bringin' Up Old Shit? 165

Chapter 18: Google Doesn't Always Have the Answers You Need 173

Part 4: Make Yourself Big 185

Chapter 19: Make It 'til You Make It 191

Chapter 20: Your Tribe Affects Your Vibe 203

Chapter 21: REAL Talk 211

Part 5: Embracing the Bossing Up Life 223

Chapter 22: Bro, Do You Even Lift? 227

Chapter 23: Trust Me, You Can Afford It 233

Chapter 24: A Balanced Life Is Overrated 243

Chapter 25: #Winning 253

Chapter 26: Prepare to Get Schooled 261

Chapter 27: You Might Suck 275

Chapter 28: There Is No Finish Line 287

Extra Tips for Those Who Are Bossing Up 293

The Bossing Up Manifesto 299

Thank You 301

A Peek Behind the Curtain of My Procrastinating Mind 303

Bibliography 311

Links 317

Reasons for wanting to Boss Up

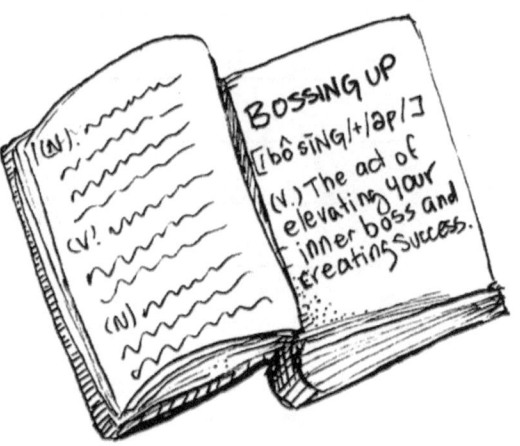

Bossing Up Defined

Bossing Up

/bôsiNG/ + /əp/

The act of harnessing your hunger and creating success.

A true boss knows their worth, wants him/herself and others to succeed, and does whatever it takes to make it happen.

Prelude

Bossing Up is a collection of stories, advice, and actionable tools that I used to earn five promotions in five years, double my salary in the process, and propel me into entrepreneurship. My story isn't one of accidental success, privilege, or luck. Every move was strategic and deliberate, and adjusted as needed as things progressed. Every step has been documented and reflected upon. Bossing Up is my blueprint for success, and I want to share it with *you*.

How you define success, much like who you are as an individual, evolves over time. It's an ongoing process, a journey with no end destination. Let's be clear here from the beginning: you won't find any shortcuts here, no bait and switch title, or false promises to make you more successful in "three easy steps." Being truly successful requires hard work and heavy lifting. With this book, my goal is to distill the onslaught of information you face every day telling you what you need to do to achieve success, and to put it all into actionable steps so that you can begin making progress today.

Do you have the capability to be successful? Yes. Is there a possibility for you to earn more, learn more, and live more in the process? Yes. Is there a proven plan to follow that will guide you to success? Yes. Is there a one-size-fits-all plan for everyone? No. However, these exact steps worked for me and many of them are followed by some of the most successful people I know. Read the plan, personalize it according to your goals, and practice Bossing Up. Success will follow.

My Bossing Up Journey

I come from a hardworking, middle-class family. I never wanted for anything, but I learned early on that everything we had was earned, nothing was given. I had a happy childhood, loving parents, and I lived in a safe part of town. I was in grade school when my best friend, Sarah, at eleven years old, went missing. Too young, innocent, and naïve to the dangers outside of the life my parents had created for me, I didn't comprehend how something like that could happen. After what seemed like an eternity seeking to find her, we were given the news that she wouldn't be coming home. My family was shaken. She was a victim of an unspeakable crime, of which only later in life did I learn the details. As I grew older, I became determined to not let her death be in vain, and I enrolled in the Youth and Adult Correctional Intervention program. I wanted to understand criminals. I thought that by knowing why and how they're capable of committing awful crimes, I could help people at risk of taking the same path.

I was nineteen years old and fresh out of college when, upon completion of my internship, I was hired at a live-in rehabilitation facility. I began my career as an addictions counselor. I was still a kid, but there I was, holding focus groups and trying to help patients battling battle demons older than I was. As the rookie, I was put on the night shift. There were no locks on the doors, no cameras, and a house full of people who would've rather been anywhere else. I was getting paid under the table, so with no record of me working there, nights were particularly stressful.

One night, I sat across from a man who wanted to up and leave. I couldn't force him to stay, but it was my job to convince him to stay at least until morning, when his dedicated counselor returned. He sat there calmly, looking down at his hands as he rubbed them together, slowly. He brought his left arm to his right shoulder, pulled up his sleeve and asked, "Do you see this sun tattoo on my arm?"

"Yes," I responded.

He replied, "Each ray of sun represents a person I've killed." He continued, "The therapy is just not working. I feel nothing. I have nothing left."

After a long and humbling conversation, he decided to stay through the night and went to sleep while I tried to digest what had just happened. This was *it*. *This* was the kind of moment I got into the field for. But I didn't feel happy or accomplished. I didn't even feel scared. I felt hollow.

The months that followed that conversation were life-changing for both of us. With the intervention of his counselor, he completed therapy and began to change. He was happy: he was trying to better himself and he had hope for a brighter future. As for me, I grew tired, my stress levels skyrocketed, and I felt anxious every time I walked into work. It became painfully obvious that I didn't want to pursue a career in the correctional field. I felt that my years of schooling had gone to waste. I felt that I had no purpose. I felt that I was failing Sarah. I felt the unreasonable responsibility to save everyone and make the world a better place, and was being crushed by that pressure. The morning I decided to resign I remembered reading a report years earlier that claimed, before going missing, Sarah was saving her babysitting money to visit family in Florida. She was a dreamer, with great ambition, the desire to experience all that life had to offer, and she would've wanted that for me.

After a lifetime of ambition and only two short years in the field, I decided to work for a local school board as I finished my university degree. I thought about careers that I could have that wouldn't feel like work. Ones that would be fun, that closely aligned with my hobbies and interests, and that would make me excited to go to work every day. I'd love to tell you that I put a lot of thought into this decision, but truthfully, I decided to make a drastic career change with no more than one conversation and a couple of Google searches. I threw caution to the wind and became a wedding planner. I did another internship, this time out of personal interest rather than for school. I worked alongside one of the city's most talented planners and soaked in as much information as I could. I was networking, managing projects, organizing, being creative, and I got to let my girly flag fly; some of my favorite things. It was a refreshing change and I felt entirely in my element. I eventually went out on my own; I started with planning small, intimate weddings and then moved onto elaborate half-million-dollar weddings. I was the embodiment of every wedding planner portrayed in the movies, complete with clipboard, headset, and mini fires to put out (including a *literal* one, moments before the bride arrived), and I *loved* it… the wedding planning, not the firefighting duties. More than the love stories, the flowers, and the endless supply of desserts I took home each night, I got a taste of the entrepreneurial life and I'd never felt more empowered.

I went on to plan events on my own and after a couple of years of playing fairy godmother to brides-to-be, an unexpected opportunity presented itself that was rather tempting. A well-known entertainment company was hiring a marketing coordinator to lead its offline events. I weighed my options and thought, what if I were to decide eventually to leave the world of event planning and I were to reach my thirties with no corporate experience? So, to offset the risk of not looking traditionally employable on my resume, and to pursue my genuine interest in this opportunity, I decided to go for the interview. I may have had no formal marketing training, but I did have more than sixty plus events under my belt. I had even done a few bridal shows that gave me some, albeit minimal, experience with print, radio, and social media advertising; it wasn't a perfect match, but my limited knowledge paired with my boundless confidence was enough to secure their attention and get my foot in the door. After a grueling month-long waiting period, I was pleased to learn that I was offered the job. I remember getting the call as I was about to begin my Intro to Italian exam, my last exam before graduating university.

I started my new role the very next day. I went from being a student to a professional marketer overnight. I was like a sponge. I soaked in everything I could, learning as much as I could off the clock as I did during my nine to five. When I discovered I was good at marketing, I thought, *Amazing, THIS must be what I'm meant to do!* I went all in. And my efforts were recognized. I earned Top Performer on my first review, and the seed to strive for success was planted. I wanted more. I was hungry and I had no intention of losing that appetite. I wanted to climb the corporate ladder all the way to the top. So, I started climbing. I took every opportunity to grow professionally and personally. I took every course and rose to every challenge. As a result, I never got through a full stack of business cards with my new title before my next promotion.

I was living the good life. My team and my department continued to grow, achieving milestone after milestone. I travelled the world and mingled with some of the top names in business. I went from sitting at my cubicle, no more than a spec on upper management's radar, to attending yacht parties in France with the executive team. I didn't rise in rank because of any particular privilege; I was not well-connected going into this role. But I had ferocious determination and undeniable hustle. I was hungry, I worked hard, and I made every effort to make improvements every single day. I earned my spot at the table (or boat).

By the time I completed my fifth year in marketing, I had earned five promotions and my salary had doubled from the day I started. I was having the time of my life, but despite the luxuries that came with the job, I recognized that, in five short years, my role had grown to all it could be in that company. I felt too young to be stagnant in my career.

So, once again I decided to hit the drawing board and consider my next steps. My friends and family thought I was crazy for giving up such an incredible position, but I couldn't stay there knowing that I had already peaked. My idea of success had evolved. It was no longer about the lavish dinner parties (although they were a nice perk), it was about the sense of fulfillment that came from conquering a new challenge: I enjoyed the process of evolving. And with nothing substantial left to conquer and with no challenge left to facilitate any future growth, I began my hunt for something more.

Did you hear that? I could swear I just heard someone mutter "typical millennial" under their breath.

I put some serious thought into what would make me happy and what would present me with the new challenges I craved. All signs pointed to the same direction: it was time to bring my dream of starting my own business to life. I started to dream big. I thought about my company name, my different skill sets, and the possibility of working from anywhere in the world—I was high on the entrepreneurial hype. I purchased a domain name and a website theme, got some professional photos taken, and was ready! Then my logic kicked in (thanks for passing that gene down, dad!) and I took my head out of the clouds just long enough to realize that I didn't have any money saved, and I wouldn't be able to pay my rent with wit alone.

That didn't stop me, though. It just became part of the plan. Instead of quitting my job and living on a prayer, I thought about the skills I lacked and wanted to refine before venturing out on my own. With the intention of getting a better grasp on demand generation, negotiation, and brand storytelling, I set my sights on a start-up digital marketing agency and gave myself one year to get entrepreneur-ready. I put a few bucks aside and learned everything I could.

Choosing to move to a start-up environment was one of the best strategic decisions I ever made. It was only then that I learned to truly appreciate what hustling meant and how critical it is to a start-up's success. Unfortunately, in that company, the hustle was completely lacking and was the eventual cause of its demise. Every day there was a rollercoaster: new business was hard to come by and fear of failure fueled every decision from upper management. I got a crash course in entrepreneurship and learned very quickly how *not* to run a business. Nevertheless, every day came with a new lesson that fuelled my desires to pursue my ambition of running my own company.

My motivation was not to ditch the nine to five or to be my own boss: I wanted a steady flow of new challenges to conquer that would facilitate my professional and personal growth. Now, as a success coach, I'm always learning about new markets, industries, philosophies, and everything in between. Clients seek my help overcoming challenges in their own professional and personal lives, which ensures my job is never redundant or boring. I have created my ideal job and I just so happen to be my own boss. I must admit, it's a pretty great set-up.

I enjoyed the office life and I still appreciate the structure and opportunities that the corporate world provides, but I feel that entrepreneurship was in my cards from an early age. My early memories bear this out.

In a recent conversation with one of my sisters, we reminisced about our childhoods and laughed about the many times we played together in the basement. We couldn't have been older than seven, and when my sister's turn would come to choose the game, we would line up our Barbie dolls and teddy bears and play "law." We each represented our clients (mine was usually Mr. Sparkles), and we'd have to plead our cases. Mine, unknowingly, tended to be based on circumstantial evidence—a word I could barely pronounce at the time—and I often lost.

When it was my turn to decide the game, I would choose for us to strategize our next business opportunity. I had big plans for us to run the playground, and eventually the neighborhood. We made bracelets, pet rocks, Christmas cards, and new (read: awful) flavors of soda by combining whatever was in the fridge. We planned to sell all of this at the park, at the pool, and even door-to-door if we had to. I was far from being a bona fide business woman, but my entrepreneurial intent was present from the beginning. Today, my sister is a respected lawyer, and I've harnessed my entrepreneurial hunger into a business that I'm proud of.

My professional journey has been unusual, to say the least. I get that. But that's what makes Bossing Up so rad. It isn't a way of life exclusively for aspiring or current entrepreneurs. It's for those who are hungry for more, and who have stepped up to the plate and decided they're going to be their best selves. Being a Boss isn't necessarily about picking one thing and dedicating yourself to it until you've achieved all that you can. Being a Boss is about growing and learning who you are. It's about realizing when changes need to be made and being courageous enough to make them. Bossing Up is about living up to your true potential and discovering new capabilities in yourself you didn't even know were hiding. And it's about helping others to do the same so that we leave behind a planet of empowered and happy people.

No matter what you do, regardless of your title, or what path you've taken to get you where you are now, if you want to create success and live a life you're proud of, this book is for you. My blueprint is by no means the holy grail of success, but it has worked for me and for others who have taken the same steps. So, take what you need, leave what you don't. Develop your own blueprint and live by it.

Success Stoppers

I work with young professionals fresh on the scene, CEOs, and everyone in between. They all want to succeed. While their definitions of success may vary, they all have one thing in common: they sometimes get stuck. And that's where I come in. Being stuck often boils down to a lack of confidence, a lack of resourcefulness, and an abundance of fear, all of which makes it difficult to succeed. Being stuck feels oppressive and overwhelming. It's frustrating and saps your inspiration, yet it's actually a blessing in disguise. Feeling stuck is a symptom of mundane behavior that tells us that change is needed. It's your brain's way of telling you that your old ways of doing things aren't cutting it anymore. Whether you require a change of heart, a change of priorities, or a change of perspective, something's gotta give.

"If you don't like something, change it. If you can't change it, change your attitude." - Maya Angelou

Throughout my experiences, I've recognized five common themes that get in the way of success. I call them *success stoppers*:

1. We don't know what we want.
2. We believe we want what others want and pursue their imposed success.
3. We focus on perfection instead of progress.
4. We keep ourselves small.
5. We compromise our definition of success based on fear.

If you're experiencing one or more of these success stoppers, there's nothing wrong with you. It's hard to move beyond what's stopping you if you don't fully understand what it is and how it got there. We all get stuck at some point in our lives; it's inevitable, but staying stuck isn't. Success stoppers flatline your motivation. But rest assured, motivation can be revived.

Bossing Up is inspired by these success stoppers and this book will give you the tools you need to face your obstacles, overcome them, and embrace success.

Notes

KNOW WHAT you WANT

Part 1: Know What You Want

Many of us are in a perpetual state of "stuckness" because we haven't identified what we want, let alone actively pursued it.

We all know someone (or have been *that* someone) who's working a dead-end job, who chooses to stay in an unfulfilling relationship, or who's waiting for the clouds to part and send down a sign that will lead them to their true calling. People in this state go through the motions, but are rarely satisfied with their lives. They're on autopilot and have become too acquainted with the warm and fuzzy feeling of their routine to do anything about it. Most times, it's not for a lack of wanting more. They just feel lost with no direction and no idea how to get onto the right path.

Getting onto the right path for *you* starts by identifying your desires. Discovering what makes you happy requires hard work. And you must *show up* for this work to get done, just like you must show up for any job. I always say the first step to Bossing Up is showing up. Even if it seems pointless at first, you've got to show up for yourself day in, day out. You must be open to seeing and doing things differently, however big or small the action.

When you know what you want, when you *really* know what you *really* want, you've got to stick to the landing in order to get unstuck. Throughout this book, you'll read stories of fellow bosses taking small actions toward big dreams. We often hear stories of the people who have made it and the struggles they've endured to get where they are. While we may admire them, the glitz and glamour of their lifestyles can be somewhat unrelatable. The "Bossing Up in Action" stories are of bosses, just like you, who are in the process of elevating their inner Boss in real time. They represent the daily grind, and the hard choices and emotional rollercoasters that we're all experiencing.

Bossing Up in Action

Michelle Manzione, ABC 7News, Washington, D.C

Michelle had lived in Florida her entire life, but when an opportunity became available to join ABC News in Washington as an intern, she up and left the only life she knew. Pursuing a lifelong dream of working in the media, Michelle moved to one of the most expensive cities in the United States where she made little more than minimum wage. With a Master's Degree and a 300-square foot studio apartment, Michelle's ego took a hit, but it didn't knock her down. Through positive affirmations, hard work, and the willingness to seize every opportunity, Michelle was promoted to a managerial position in less than a year. Knowing what she wanted and going for it was the best decision she ever made.

Her advice to you:

> *"Find out what you're passionate about, go after it, and do not give up."*

People who get what they want are those who make the effort to know what that is. Here's how to get started.

> *"You can't find what you want if you don't know what you're looking for."* - Matthew E. Freyer

Notes

Chapter 1
I'm All Ears

The Impact Listening Has on Success

Many of us spend 70 to 80 percent of our waking hours communicating in one form or another. Of that time, we spend roughly 9 percent writing, 16 percent reading, 30 percent speaking, and 45 percent *listening*. Think about it: whether you're in class, in a meeting, or tuned into a podcast, an audio book, a movie, or a conversation, *listening* is your most utilized communication skill. But how effective are you as a listener?

Don't mistake hearing for listening. Effective listening isn't a passive task: it's an active process that enables us to make sense of, assess, and respond to what we hear. It may take effort to master, but effective listening is critical to our success. It allows us to build and maintain relationships; to learn and to grow; to maximize our productivity; and to develop confidence in our ability to achieve our goals. Effective listening helps you to reflect on the information that's available to you, and enables you to form your own opinions. Effective listening allows you to become a better thinker and communicator, which ultimately helps you to discover what you really want.

I've got to admit, I'm a great listener. Not to toot my own horn here, but it's one of my strong suits. I wasn't always a great listener, though. I was a stubborn kid, determined to learn everything on my own. I didn't want any help and I didn't need to listen to anyone …yeah right. My listening skills developed accidentally when I made a new friend who was hard of hearing.

I sat beside her in fourth grade and every time she missed something the teacher had said, she would subtly place her hand on the corner of my desk and I'd repeat it for her. I had convinced myself that I wasn't listening because *I wanted to*, I was *listening for her*. I actually totally loved it though. I pretended that I was a spy collecting top secret information, or a reporter covering a story that relied heavily on intricate details. As part of the game, I wrote down whatever I could remember. I began journaling what I learned, what people's reactions were, and any additional things I could observe. So, ten-year-old-me didn't have all the answers after all! Listening then became an integral part of all the relationships in my life and I got to know people differently from how others knew them. I couldn't really explain it at the time, but even so, I knew that I was onto something special. I liked the way it made me feel, as well as how it made others feel. That feeling is what led me to do my bachelor's degree in Human Relations, the ultimate "life skills" program. It essentially teaches students how to relate to people. Who couldn't benefit from that? I spent years learning the dynamics of group and one-on-one interactions, from families to corporations.

I still don't have all the answers, but I did learn a thing or two. I'll spare you the four years of classes and share the CliffsNotes to becoming a better listener.

The active listening process is broken down into five stages: receiving, understanding, remembering, evaluating, and responding, as follows:

1. **Receiving.** Pay attention to *how* someone is communicating, as much as, if not more than, the *words* they're using. Process their tone and body language in order to distill what they're expressing. To make sure you're picking up on all the cues, give them your full attention. Don't listen to respond—your turn will come—listen to understand.

2. **Understanding.** It's easy to forget and disengage from conversations that we don't understand. Effective communication occurs when you understand the speaker, and the best way to ensure you've understood correctly is to ask questions, and then to paraphrase or summarize what they've just said. This will help to keep you engaged, retain the information you've just received, and better prepare you for a response.

3. **Remembering.** In his lecture, "Study less, study smart," Psychology Professor Dr. Marty Lobdell, tells us that our ability to retain information diminishes after twenty-five to thirty minutes. Studies show that, on average, we retain 90 percent of what we learn when we ourselves teach a new concept to someone else or when we immediately put it into practice. Although you will not likely spontaneously find yourself in a position to teach others what you've just learned yourself, thinking about how you could explain it to someone, or how you could put it into practice, will help you to retain the information better and longer.

4. **Evaluating.** Once you've absorbed, understood, and retained the information, you're ready to start thinking about how you want to respond. Acknowledge the speaker's

intent, knowledge, and demeanor, and prepare to respond in a way that will elicit a deeper conversation (or end the conversation if you're not feeling it).

5. **Responding.** Recall the most important points that were made in the context of the situation at hand and address them in a fluid manner to avoid coming off as confrontational. While you're not in response mode, you should constantly repeat the active listening process as the conversation progresses.

This might seem like a lot to think about in a short period of time, but these steps take seconds to employ and can potentially reverse years of bad communication habits. Since listening accounts for the bulk of your communication, and communication is vital to your success, it's in your best interest to brush up on your listening skills. If you're not convinced, consider this: we listen to learn, to stay informed, and to better connect with others. It's the single most important tool for success, yet it often goes forgotten and it's something that many are not particularly good at. Refining it will give you a competitive advantage in business and in life. It helps you to:

Build better relationships. Dale Carnegie, bestselling author of *How to Win Friends and Influence People* said, "You can make more friends in 2 weeks by becoming a good listener than you can in 2 years trying to get other people interested in you." Listening to others and making an effort to understand their perspective shows them that you care. When they recognize that you're invested in what they have to say, they feel important. And when they feel important, they will want to keep you around.

Be smarter. This is probably not a huge surprise. The more you listen, the more you know, and the more you know, the smarter you are. Duh. It also helps you to generate new ideas. Inspiration is everywhere, but you must constantly be on the lookout. Effective listening can help you to uncover the missing link in a project that you've been stuck on, or to uncover your next big idea.

Be real with yourself. Not everything you listen to is going to be earth-shattering knowledge that will change your life. Oftentimes, you'll hear things you've heard before and have a, *Yeah, I know that already* reaction. But common sense isn't always common practice. Hearing it again, in a different context, may be just what you need in order to reflect on why you're struggling to make progress and kick you into high gear.

Earn respect. When you're not fully present, when you listen only to respond, or when you hijack the conversation to talk only about yourself, you're sending a strong message that you don't care about what the other person is saying. Trying to be impressive and interesting to others won't earn you the respect that you're looking for. Instead, show the person you're talking to that you value what they're saying by being impressed and interested. People appreciate that behavior and will often extend the same courtesy to you when you have something you want to share with them. The respect established through effective listening puts you at the forefront of their minds for future opportunities.

Make an impact. The more words you use, the more you dilute your message. Listening allows you to think through your thoughts and formulate a response that allows you to quickly get to your point. The less runaround you have to undergo to effectively express yourself, the easier it will be to get the buy-in of those listening.

Being an active listener has helped me to avoid misunderstandings and unnecessary arguments. It has allowed me to pick up on subtleties in body language and in tone, and to guide the conversation into the direction that I want it to go. It has also improved my overall ability to communicate, enabling me to accomplish what I set out to achieve.

"No one is as deaf as the man who will not listen." – Proverb

Notes

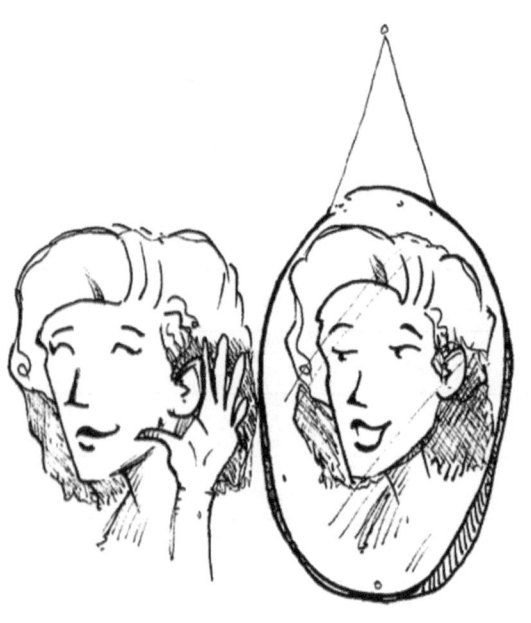

Chapter 2
The Woman in the Mirror

*Listen to Yourself, It Might Be the Best Advice
You'll Ever Receive*

Listening to what others have to say is beneficial to discovering what you want, but listening to yourself will allow you to pursue success on your own terms. Listening to yourself starts with hearing yourself; you must be open to receiving what your body and mind are telling you, even when you don't like what they're saying.

About two years before starting my business, I began experiencing an awful pain in my stomach. Sitting down hurt, standing up hurt, and everything I ate left me in pain. I was vomiting regularly with little to no warning. I underwent tests for crohn's disease, celiac disease, IBS, you name it. They all came back negative. The doctors were stumped. As far as they could see, I was perfectly healthy, but I knew something was wrong, very wrong. I knew what it was, but I refused to acknowledge it.

I'm stubborn and have a high tolerance to stress. While I was fully on board with maintaining a positive, conscious mindset, I disregarded the effects of a negative *subconscious*, and refused to believe that the pain I was experiencing was stress-related. I had read all about the power of the mind, but surely stress wasn't what was taking *me* down. I was stronger than that.

The truth was, I was in a marriage that was preventing me from achieving my full potential. While it was a wonderful and loving relationship for a long time, the more I learned about myself, the more I realized what I was capable of, and wanted to be more than a wife. The more confident I became in my professional life, the more opportunities became available to me. I wanted to explore them all. I didn't want to leave any stone unturned. Yet every opportunity pulled me further away from the partner I had promised to be. The idea of having children and a house in the suburbs, once my ideal future, now suffocated me. I wanted to live in the city and see how high I could climb up the corporate ladder. I wanted to see what other opportunities were waiting for me. But I knew that asking my then-husband to put his dreams of having a family on hold even longer for me was unfair.

I felt selfish and conflicted. I projected strength and determination to my outer world, but I was a total mess internally. How could I do this to him? Why couldn't I just be happy with what I had? Deep down (and I mean *deep* down), I knew why this was such a struggle. I knew that listening inward would trigger the demise of my marriage, and that was too much to face; so, I chose not to face it. Refusing to listen inwardly was rooted partially in denial and partially in fear, but it was *wholly* taking over my subconscious and literally destroying me from the inside out. One of my most sobering experiences was learning that I was not invincible. When my health had deteriorated to the point that I no longer felt like myself, I accepted that I needed to hear what my body was telling me. I began to listen.

I heard the voice of a strong woman who sounded like me, but she was distant, as if she was miles away; so, it was hard to tell if this was indeed my voice. The more I listened, the closer she got, and I finally found the strength I thought I'd lost. My inner voice told me that it's okay to change, there's no shame in growing, and that things would work out in the end as long as I continued to listen inwardly. So, I did, and every time things felt like they weren't working out, I reminded myself that whatever current situation was troubling me was simply not the end of the world. It was a long and trying process, but it became evident that my marriage shouldn't last. Parting ways has been one of the hardest things I've ever experienced, but it has allowed me to step into my true self.

I have since rerouted my journey and started over. With not much in my bank account and just a couple of pieces of furniture in my possession, I moved to the city and embraced the new me. I said yes to all interesting opportunities, guilt-free. I got my health back on track and discovered an appreciation for the physical effects of my mental well-being on my body. I launched a business that provides me with a profound sense of fulfillment in helping others succeed. I've written my first book (thanks for reading it, by the way!) which has been a long-time goal of mine. And I've carved out more time for traveling, including a particularly exciting trip with an incredible group of ladies to educate and empower a community of women in Accra, Ghana; an international philanthropic experience and a trip to Africa were both personal bucket list items of mine.

There's truly no shortage of possibilities open to you if you're willing to listen to yourself. Believe it or not, you have all the answers you need *internally* to make success a reality. These are the steps I took to strengthen my inner communication, and how you can too:

1. **Create a safe place for listening.** I've got a favorite wingback chair that's my preferred place for listening. The armrests are at the perfect height for me to rest my knees when sitting cross-legged. The chair supports perfect posture, the wings feel like a familiar and loving hug, and the chair faces a window that lets in natural light. In this chair, I feel as if I'm the captain of my life ship, fortified by clear direction and purpose. You must find a place for yourself where you can reach such tranquility. It doesn't matter if this is in your car, on your porch, or in the crawlspace underneath the stairs. Find a place where you can disconnect from everything that oppresses you and where you can declutter your mind. Try to enjoy your own company without technology or books, and see where your mind takes you.

2. **When you're stuck, think about the five W's.** It's fascinating how we can have a "don't ask, don't tell" relationship with ourselves. We may think, *Oh, if I don't think about it then it won't bother me*, but that couldn't be further from the truth. My story about how I came to listen to myself is proof of that; our bodies express themselves physically (and I mean *unpleasantly*) when we ignore what our minds and hearts are trying to tell us. So, when something seems too daunting to contemplate, I break it down into manageable thoughts. I first learned to not overthink things when I worked at the rehabilitation center. You've probably heard of the KISS method. There are several interpretations of this acronym, but the one that left a lasting impact on me was, *Keep It Simple, Stupid*. It's not particularly motivational, but it forces you to think of other

ways to tackle a seemingly big task without overcomplicating it.

I tend to get caught up in the minutia of my life, so, I have to consciously make time to check in with myself to make sure I'm on the right track. But I'm not always in the mood for a super deep internal monologue, so, I settle into my favorite chair and keep it simple by turning to the five W's I learned in grade school to help me identify:

1. **Who** will my decisions impact?
2. **What** can I do to improve my situation?
3. **When** did I start feeling this way and **when** will I take action?
4. **Where** do I see myself in six months?
5. **Why** do I feel this way?

Oftentimes, a quick listening session does the trick, and I'm able to pinpoint what my success stopper is, what I need to do to fix it, and how fixing it (or not fixing it) will impact me and those around me. It's a simple and powerful way to take back control. Give it a shot, what's the best that could happen?

3. **Don't stop asking yourself questions.** You might think that you're doing yourself a favor by just going with the flow and taking things as they come, but be careful. While the willingness and ability to adapt in life is important, if you never stop to ask yourself what you want, you may never get it. Questions don't need to be reserved for moments of "stuckness." Regularly asking yourself

questions is a healthy practice that allows you to tune into yourself and to make sure that you're not asleep at the wheel. Niurka, creator of Supreme Influence, claims that the quality of our lives is determined by the questions that we ask. Language and communication play a critical role in how we listen to both others and to *ourselves*. The language you use to find answers to your internal questions should reflect the context of your current situation; this gives momentum to your questions and better allows you to make positive changes.

Niurka encourages people to ask themselves, *why am I doing this?* Acknowledge if you're doing it to move *towards* something or to *avoid* something. If it's the latter, you may notice that once you're far enough away, your subconscious can begin to sabotage you. For example, if you're moving *away* from being overweight, you'll likely think that you can start eating anything you want again once you've lost the weight. Whereas if you're looking to move *towards* a healthier lifestyle, you'll have a better change are creating a sustainable positive change. You will get what you ask for. Be specific because if it's not what you're looking for, it's not what you'll see.

4. **Treat yourself as you would treat others.** The "Golden Rule" we're taught when we're young is to treat others the way we want to be treated ourselves. Well, I'm flipping that on its head. We tend to criticize ourselves more than anyone else, and we're often our own worst critic. I know I would never treat others the way I have often treated myself. Don't use this time of self-reflection to beat yourself up. Be kind, be patient, and allow yourself time to

figure out the answers you seek. Be an effective listener to yourself. Absorb what your mind, body, and soul are telling you. Try to understand where your answers are coming from and remember as much as you can. Our thoughts fly by at a rapid pace, so make a note in an app, do a quick voice note, or whip out your journal, but remember all you can for future reflection and evaluation. Above all, be compassionate in your responses. The way you communicate with yourself will directly affect your mood and will become part of your self-talk the next time you're faced with a challenge. It can make or break your chances for success.

5. **Be aware of warning signs.** I'm going to speak for a minute to all the workaholics in the family. You. Yes, YOU. Remember this: nobody makes it to their deathbed wishing they had spent more time at the office. Nobody is immune to burnout, and this doesn't apply exclusively to your professional life. Anyone who is passionate and identifies as an over-achiever is equally at risk. If you're putting an immense amount of pressure on yourself, it's critical to know when you need a break. Whether you take a vacation, spend the day at the spa, plan a date night, or give yourself permission to just do nothing (GASP!), you need to take care of yourself. As the saying goes, you can't pour from an empty cup. So, don't let the cup go empty, and avoid burning out by listening to what your mind and body are saying.

When I ignore the signals my body and mind are sending me, my fire begins to dim, and it impacts every area of my life. Warning signs for me are typically a lack of, or an increase in, appetite, as well as stress dreams, dehydration, and increased irritability. Other warning signs can include, but are not limited to, physical and emotional exhaustion, pessimism, detachment, forgetfulness, inexplicable physical symptoms, a weak immune system, and anxiety. If this sounds familiar, walk up to a mirror and say, *Hey, what have you got to tell me?*

Full disclosure: this is much tougher than it seems. I'm often reminded that I need to spend more time listening inward and it's something I'm actively working on. This is by no means "five easy steps to listen to yourself"; it's *hard* work. But turning your listening skills inwardly is one of the most effective ways to reduce stress, increase personal happiness, and identify what you want. It will guide you, empower you to make better decisions, and lead you to success. You may still make mistakes, but your mistakes *won't make you.*

"Listen to yourself, not the noise of the world. Only you know what is right for you." - Leon Brown

Notes

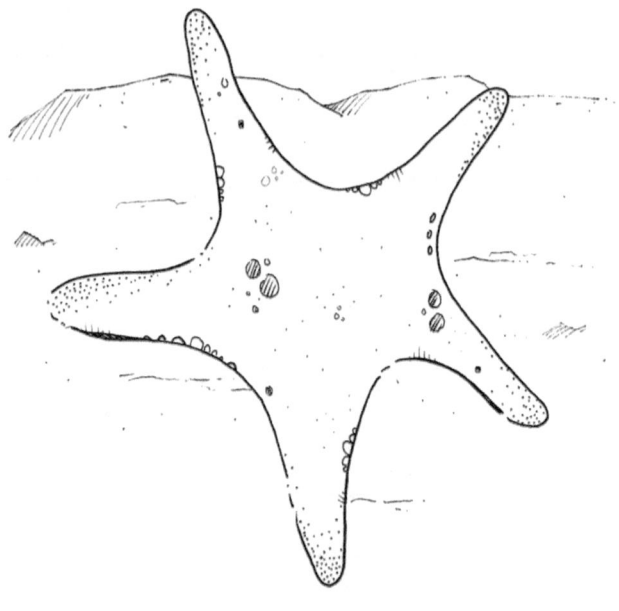

Chapter 3
Car Crashes, Canyons, and Sharks

There's a First Time for Everything

I attribute much of my success to being open to opportunity. Any speaking gig I've landed was a direct result of attending a new workshop or conference, or of taking initiative and introducing myself to someone new. Every promotion I earned was because I tried something new or offered a new perspective and consequently brought my department to new heights. Notice the theme of "new" here? You won't get better results with the same old tactics... if you think you will, you're insane (I'm not joking, folks, that is actually the definition of insanity). You've got to push the limits of your comfort zone to get unstuck and to experience growth.

Some of my best memories and wildest stories have come from stepping out of my comfort zone, like the time I jumped out of a plane in Cuba. Just a few short months earlier, I had been in a traumatic car accident. I ran my yellow light while the other driver ran a red, and our cars hit at seventy-five miles an hour. I vividly remember the second our cars collided. I saw the bright lights coming at me, but I couldn't stop fast enough. Perhaps I knew instinctively that this wasn't the end for me, but I didn't see my life flash before my eyes. Instead, my exact thought was, *Hopefully this is the most intense game of bumper cars I will ever play.*

The airbag knocked me unconscious; I don't know how long I was out. When I regained consciousness, I reached for my phone to call 911. They asked me if my car was leaking any fluid, but I didn't know, as I was still in the driver's seat. I was instructed to get out of the car immediately; I tried, but had difficulty. I didn't realize at the time that my ankle was broken and stuck under the break peddle. I didn't realize that my fingers and wrist were fractured, or that the steering wheel was pressed up against my chest because my car had been compressed like an accordion. Still on the phone with 911, they asked me if the other driver was okay. When I looked up, I saw his car, but I didn't see him. I imagined he had flown through his windshield, and I panicked. I somehow squeezed my way out of what was left of my car and ran towards his, still unaware that my ankle was broken, and not feeling any pain. I got to his car and noticed that although he wasn't in it, his windshield was still intact. I turned to find him walking behind me and talking on his cell phone. The moment I saw he was okay, the adrenaline and shock wore off and the pain from my injuries flooded my body. It took six months for me to heal. I was out of my cast only a few days before deciding to go to Cuba. Grateful for being alive, I wanted to celebrate by doing something new and exciting (read: potentially life threatening). I decided it was as good of a time as any to try skydiving. Naturally.

There was also the time I went bungee jumping off a canyon in the Swiss Alps. This was during my high school graduation trip to Europe. I would soon be going off to college with no idea of what I wanted to do or where my future would take me. I felt lost and small and I knew that wasn't how I wanted to start the next chapter of my life. I wanted to feel on top of the world, so, I signed up for bungee jumping because it was an excursion that would bring me to the highest of altitudes. A bus ride, elevator lift, and small hike later, I stood on a glass ledge that couldn't have been more than three square feet. I saw the canyon beneath me, with jagged rocks at the bottom. I decided to look up instead, and it felt as though I stood among the clouds. I was on top of the world.

I couldn't bring myself to step off the ledge, but it was the only way down. I asked the instructor to push me and he agreed to on the count of three. One ….t-PUSH. I fell from the sky for eight seconds before I reached the end of the rope. It was the most invigorating and terrifying eight seconds of my life (this was before the car crash). Time seemed to speed up and slow down at the same time. I remember thinking to myself that no matter where life takes me, the top is always within my reach.

Or the time I went swimming with sharks in the Caribbean Sea. I didn't particularly *want* to swim with sharks, but it was the cheapest activity …I wonder why …but I thought that at least the adventure would make a cool story. I was hesitant but eventually stepped into the roped-off area near the shore, where two sharks were swimming around. This probably should've been the first red flag but hey, YOLO. I immediately wanted to get out, but before I knew it, I was holding one's tail while the instructor held its head and anxiously waited for my picture to be taken. The other shark circled us, as sharks are known to do. The instructor told me calmly to get out of the water, but the picture hadn't yet been taken, so, I pretended to not have heard him (what was that about being a good listener?). He then *yelled* at me to get out of the water. When a man with a shark in his hand yells at you, you *listen* (this should totally be on a bumper sticker). As I swam away, I noticed that the other shark had bit the instructor's ankle and there was blood in the water. In case you haven't seen *Jaws*, blood in the water is a bad sign.

The lesson here: Sharks will always be around waiting to bite at your ankles; listen to your instincts.

Every time I've tried something new, I've learned something about myself. Not all new experiences need to be adrenaline-filled. Every small action counts, is accumulated and contributes to your success; it's like compound interest. With each new experience has come a discovery; strengths, fears, and desires that have all, in one way or another, shaped who I am, what I want, and my ambition to get it.

By stepping out of my comfort zone, I've learned that networking is one of my favorite pastimes and that I really enjoy public speaking (and I don't suck at it—bonus!). I've developed confidence in my ability to grow a team, a department, and myself; in other words, I've developed a strong sense of leadership. I've also experienced what it means to feel truly alive, ironically, while sometimes facing deadly circumstances. I've come to discover that I want to feel that sense of value, certainty, and fearlessness in my daily life. Any new journey I embark on, personally or professionally, must meet those needs.

You don't have to be a public speaker, manager, or adrenaline junkie to try something new. Test the waters by trying things that make sense to you. Is there a painting class you've been wanting to try? A trip you've always wanted to take? A webinar you've wanted to host? Whatever it is, do it! What's the best that could happen?

Trying new things helps you to identify what you want to experience in the following ways:

1. **Experiencing new opportunities allows you to enjoy new things.** Everything you know and love was new at some point. Think about the first time you rode a bike, your first kiss, your first trip. They may have been awkward experiences at first, and maybe a little scary, but weren't they exciting? Think about how exhilarating each experience was, how the inner voice of reassurance told you, once it was all over, *Hey, that wasn't so bad. In fact, I kind of loved it!*

   When did you decide that you were tired of firsts? Why have you stopped letting them in? It doesn't matter who you are or what your story is, everyone wants to enjoy life. And there's so much in this world to enjoy. Even though you're an adult, that feeling of exhilaration is still possible, and so is the awkwardness! Opening yourself up to trying new things can illuminate the corners of your mind that have been waiting to see the light. New passions, hobbies, career opportunities, and entirely new lifestyles can be discovered by stepping outside the box you've mentally confined yourself to.

2. **It encourages you to trust yourself.** Many of us avoid trying new things because somewhere along the way we told ourselves that we can't do them well or at all. Our self-limiting beliefs have trained us to distrust our ability to succeed at new things. Regularly challenging yourself to do something new retrains your brain to produce self-liberating beliefs. You don't need to become an expert at your new

activity for this exercise to work; you just need to *do it*. In this case, capability = victory. Squash your "I can't" self-talk and instill self-trust by proving to yourself that you can in fact do what you put your mind to. Establishing this trust in yourself will make it easier for you to confidently go after available opportunities and to create new ones.

3. **New challenges prevent you from getting bored.** It's hard to know what you want for yourself when you're bored. Have you ever noticed that finding something to do when you're bored feels *impossible*? When I'm bored, it seems like everyone is busy, there are no good movies on Netflix, and there's really no use in starting that project I've been meaning to get to because I only have a couple of hours left before I should be going to sleep. Gross. How can you expect yourself to figure out what you want within that headspace? It's not easy, so, avoid boredom at all cost.

Boredom is not to be confused with laziness, though you should avoid falling into the lazy trap, too. You may have a lot to do and you may even get a lot done, but if you're focusing all your efforts on doing the same tasks all day, every day, your creativity and inspiration will stagnate. Even if you're hell-bent on not stepping too far outside your comfort zone, you can still explore other aspects of your job, neighborhood, or hobbies to keep life from getting monotonous. Once monotony sets in, you're as useless as I am flipping aimlessly through Netflix. No matter how you cut it, boredom is the enemy of success. You should fear being bored more than you fear failure. You can avoid letting apathy take over by keeping things new and exciting. Finding new challenges promotes personal development and will help you break free of the mundane.

Car Crashes, Canyons, and Sharks

Of course, trying new things can be nerve-wracking. Leaving the cushy walls of our habitual minds puts us in a vulnerable position of self-doubt. We start to ask ourselves, *Can I do this? What if I fail? Do I look stupid?* The answer? *So what!* So what if your painting of a starfish looks more like a murder scene? So what if booking your trip took four years longer than planned? So what if your webinar flopped? You did it, you now know whether or not it was for you, and you can make improvements for whenever you try again.

But, hey, what if you succeed? What if you discover that you're actually a very talented painter and this skill has been dormant and neglected your whole life? What if you take that long-planned trip and meet the love of your life, or have a life-changing revelation? What if your webinar is so successful that it inspires you to create other digital educational assets that go on to generate one million dollars in just over a year, and two and a half million dollars in the next two years? It happened to Lewis Howes; why can't it happen to you?

"Opportunity doesn't make appointments, you have to be ready when it arrives." - Tim Fargo

Notes

Notes

Chapter 4
What You Weren't Taught in School

How to ~~Not Be an Asshole~~ Practice Emotional Intelligence

In school, we study history, isosceles triangles, and how to dissect frogs, but nowhere in the curriculum is there a class that teaches us how to identify and manage our own emotions, or to effectively deal with the emotions of others. We're not taught about the importance of empathy, self-awareness, or appropriate social skills. I'm not sure about you, but understanding how someone is feeling and knowing how to respond to them in a helpful and nonthreatening manner has been far more useful to me than any distant memory of the Pythagorean Theorem.

Emotional intelligence isn't a new concept. The term first appeared in 1964, but has gained popularity in the last ten years. It's all the buzz, but what does being emotionally intelligent mean?

You know that colleague who's a good listener? The one who listened to you vent? The one who gave you valuable, constructive criticism in a way that resonated with you and didn't upset you? The one that was considerate of your circumstances, and who left you feeling hopeful that things would start looking up even without giving you a solution to your problem?

Or how about that friend who not only looks like they've got their shit together, but *actually* does? The one who always keeps their emotions in check and responds like a respectful adult as opposed to reacting like an undisciplined child? The one who seems to be fazed by nothing or no one, and who sees solutions rather than problems? The one who gives honest feedback and can receive it as well without getting offended?

These are the people in your network who exude high levels of emotional intelligence, or EQ (emotional quotient). They know themselves very well and can identify and manage their own emotions and behaviors, as well as the emotions and behaviors of others. They're capable of harnessing their emotions and applying them to critical thinking and problem-solving. As a result, they have an easier time navigating social complexities and tend to succeed at most things they do. This isn't because they're geniuses; it's because they make others feel good, so, people want them on their team. People genuinely want them to succeed and will help them however they can.

If you're interested in increasing your emotional intelligence and becoming someone whom others want to help achieve greater success, rest assured that this is a skill that can be learned and developed. Some of the ways you can strengthen your emotional intelligence are as follows:

Expand your emotional vocabulary. You can learn to master your emotions better when you understand them better. Travis Bradberry, co-founder of TalentSmart says, "While many people might describe themselves as simply feeling 'bad', emotionally intelligent people can pinpoint whether they feel 'irritable', 'frustrated', 'downtrodden', or 'anxious'. The more specific your word choice, the better insight you have into exactly how you're feeling, what caused it, and what you should do about it." As you begin to better associate your own feelings with specific words, the better you'll become at empathizing with others.

Become more emotionally aware. Emotional awareness is the ability to recognize when certain feelings are present in ourselves and in others, and to manage them appropriately and effectively. Pay attention to the intensity of your emotions and monitor them so that you know where you can make changes. Managing your impulses, doing things that make you happy, and being flexible to change can all contribute to strengthening your awareness. Also, strong emotional awareness helps you to be mindful of those people and environments that are toxic to you as well as those people and environments that push you to succeed. Make the conscious effort to keep negativity out and positivity in.

Be empathetic. Empathy is one of the fundamental skills of emotional intelligence. Empathetic people can put aside their views and try to understand things from the perspective of others. Refining this skill will require you to practice identifying and understanding the wants, needs, and viewpoints of those around you without judgement. Recognize how people are communicating and expressing their feelings, even when they may not be consciously trying; the ability to do so effectively will help you to better manage your relationships, become a better listener, and relate more easily to others.

Forgive yourself. We know that forgiveness frees us from bitterness and anger, yet we hold onto our self-condemnation as if it were our high school yearbook. Why? When we do something that we feel is wrong or that we regret, we register these negative emotions in our nervous system, and as a result, we feel just that: nervous, which makes it very difficult to move forward. This feeling can be massaged into something productive with a little work; the goal isn't to forget your mistakes, as you'll then likely repeat them, but rather to accept what you can't change, release any hurt that's associated with the memory of your mistakes, and use those experiences as building blocks that pave the way to success. Remember to give yourself the empathy you would give someone else.

Forgive others. Forgiveness is the decision to let things go. It doesn't mean justifying the offensive actions of others or accepting them as right. It means consciously making the choice to no longer let pain and resentment drag you down. This baggage weighs heavily on you, *not them*, and the negative emotions associated with that baggage will cloud your judgement and block you from succeeding.

Appreciate what you have. Take sixty seconds a day to think about a few things you're grateful for and write them down. Something Ralph Waldo Emerson once said that has stuck with me since I first read it is, "Watch your thoughts; they become words. Watch your words; they become actions. Watch your actions; they become habits. Watch your habits; they become character. Character is everything." Acknowledging what you're grateful for and getting it out of your head and onto paper helps manifest additional goodness.

Validate from within. People who exhibit strong emotional intelligence don't rely on praise and external support to feel good about themselves: their validation comes from within. Before seeking the approval of others, ask yourself what it is you're hoping to hear from them and tell it to yourself instead.

This practice isn't meant to deter you from reaching out to others: rather, it allows you to hear those words of encouragement and reassurance from yourself first. Hearing them from someone else becomes much more meaningful and validating when you fully believe what they're saying.

Practice self-regulation. Consciously make an effort to control your emotions and impulses. Thinking about your responses prevents you from making impulsive, careless decisions, and from saying things that you don't mean and don't want said. Having that kind of control over your thoughts, responses, and actions will help you to naturally become more thoughtful, comfortable with change, and a better communicator.

Know when to shift your focus outward. Strengthening your emotional intelligence requires a lot of internal work, but this work mustn't only occur *within* you. You must also be aware and present in the world around you. Observe your surroundings, genuinely engage with those who you encounter throughout the day, and stop to notice the sounds, scents, sights, and tastes that contribute to your experiences. Part of being emotionally intelligent is knowing what's going on both inside and outside ourselves, moment by moment.

Whether you're responsible for your team, your family, or just yourself, emotional intelligence is a critical component to happiness. If you've noticed areas that need improvement, don't fret. Unlike your IQ, raising your EQ doesn't require years of schooling and late-night study sessions, but it will require practicing new behaviors. As your brain becomes used to these behaviors and accepts them as the new normal, old habits and negative behaviors will become a thing of the past. It's a gradual and natural process that will serve you and those around you well.

> *"CEOs are hired for their intellect and business expertise - and fired for a lack of emotional intelligence." - Daniel Goleman*

Notes

Part 2: Avoid Pursuing Imposed Success

"Define success on your own terms, achieve it by your own rules, and build a life you're proud to live." - Anne Sweeney

Now that you know what you want from life, or at least know how to discover what you want, ask yourself, *what does success mean to me?* Think about it for a minute. I'm not asking you what success *looks* like by Hollywood or Instagram standards. Think about what you want and what it means to *you*. Before reading on any further, I urge you to answer this question and to hold onto your thoughts. We'll revisit this shortly.

Some people are born with an inherent purpose that is recognizable to them from the time they're in diapers. I'm happy for them, but clearly, they're not the focus of this chapter. My focus is on those who have a gut feeling about what their true calling is, but put it on the back burner in pursuit of a different path that their peers and loved ones expect them to take. My focus is also on those who have no clue what they want to do with their lives and who are struggling to find their purpose. I'd argue that most people fall into one of those two buckets.

You may have a hard time answering the question *what's my life's purpose* because you're asking the wrong question. We're here for a finite amount of time and, for the most part, we want to do things that give our lives meaning and make us happy. As self-help author Mark Manson puts it, *What will make me happy?* is an infinitely better question to ask than any other. You don't need to sell all your belongings and take a soul-searching trip to Bali, eating, praying, and loving your way to your life's purpose (though I would still strongly recommend the trip). This is a

Avoid Pursuing Imposed Success

question you can answer today. In fact, do me a solid and answer this question too, before continuing.

I know I'm asking a lot of you here, but bear with me. It's going somewhere—I promise. As a quick recap, you should have two answers stored in your ol' brain box. The questions were:

1. What does success mean to me?

2. What will make me happy?

Remember that the quality of your life is determined by the questions you ask. Aim to elicit action rather than anxiety. Asking yourself what makes you happy is manageable; it's not accompanied by the heavy baggage of "life's purpose" and it's something that you can act on immediately. At the end of the day, doing what makes you happy and pursuing your vision of success will give your life purpose anyway, right? If you're living your life based on a preconceived or imposed idea of what success is, you'll inevitably get stuck. And while you may make progress, you'll never truly be fulfilled.

So, let's put your answers to use, shall we? Does your meaning of success reflect what you think will make you happy? If there's a disconnect, dig beyond your wants. Think about what's driving them and see if it ties back to your idea of happiness. Maybe you want to make a million bucks next year. Great, but why? What do you want to *feel*?

If there's still a disconnect, or if you're uncertain of what success means to you, you may be pursuing imposed success. Imposed success is when you allow other people's vision of success to take priority over your own. It can be imposed onto you by others who are encouraging you to live a life that they want you to live, or it can be self-imposed according to the life you *think* you should be living according to society's standards of the good life. In any case, if you're pursuing goals that aren't your own, or ones that don't motivate you, you most certainly will not feel fulfilled. This next section will show you how to fix such a situation.

Notes

Chapter 5
Life's Greatest Challenge

Life's greatest challenge is discovering who you are. The second greatest challenge is liking what you find.

If you're pursuing externally-imposed definitions of success, it's not necessarily your fault. Biologically, you're wired with a sense of longing to belong. We all are. Yet there's a fundamental flaw within society that rears itself in our most vital years of childhood development and that follows us into adulthood. From a very young age, children are told that the world is their oyster while they simultaneously experience that being different from their peers is the equivalent of wearing a target on their back. They begin to fear being disliked by the other kids, and they either adapt to how they *perceive* others think they should be and bury their authenticity, or they risk being bullied for standing their ground. Those kids who morph into variations of themselves to appease others' expectations begin their high school journey with an understanding that it's better to fit in than to stand out.

Even if you've managed to avoid societal pressures as a child, by the time you reach your teenage years, the importance of internal self-validation may very well come in second behind the external validation of your friends, and your authenticity takes a backseat to conformity and to others' beliefs. It's no wonder the fear of rejection intensifies as we age and is carried by many of us into adulthood.

Fear of rejection encourages us to value others more than ourselves. It inhibits us from being truly happy or successful, and messes with our minds, tricking us into thinking that perhaps we're unlovable, unemployable, or unworthy. Fear-based thoughts encourage us to behave in ways that are misaligned with our own wants and beliefs. This often results in anxiety, known as cognitive dissonance.

You have only two options for dealing with this anxiety. You may create for yourself a life of authentic, fulfilling happiness and success. Or, you may suffer an inauthentic life of compromised, partial happiness and limited success.

Option 1: Change your behaviors so that they're aligned with your wants and beliefs.

Option 2: Tell yourself that your behavior is a reflection of your wants and beliefs, convince yourself that your actions represent who you really are, and continue to surrender to society the one thing on this earth that's uniquely yours: yourself.

Imagine had we known, as naïve and insecure kids, that in adulthood, authenticity would be our biggest and best asset! In a world filled with commodities, we now know that authenticity is vital to our success.

Being authentic goes beyond being true to ourselves, although this is an essential first step. Authenticity is a relational behavior that enables you to be who you are at your core with others. It's about continually shaping and delivering your words and actions in a way that supports your personal mission.

While I don't think I've yet solved the authenticity paradox, I have been able to align my behaviors, wants, and beliefs through these five guiding principles:

1. **Keep a journal:** Journaling allows you to observe what you want to do versus what you actually do. Identify traits and habits that align with your actions and goals. Make a note of any recurring behaviors that undermine your authenticity. Documenting these patterns allows you to reconstruct your approach to your desired actions.

2. **Live up to your ideals:** You can't just hope for change, you have to be the change. Decide who you want to become and take action. Whether it's smiling more, volunteering, working harder, or being more aware of your surroundings, you must consciously make the decision to act on your ideals.

3. **Embrace imperfection:** Own your mistakes and do what you can to make things right. Accept that you have flaws *like anyone else* but don't dwell on them. Cultivate kindness towards yourself and make progress your benchmark instead of perfection. Perfection is boring anyway.

4. **Express yourself:** Feel your emotions in their overwhelming complexity and share them. Be respectful of others, but be bold. Don't let shame, guilt, or fear guide your self-expression. Always try to express yourself from a place of compassion.

5. **Practice critical thinking:** Question your long-held beliefs and challenge your immediate responses to them. Take every opportunity to reassess your opinions to make sure

they are still aligned with your core beliefs. Resist accepting untested "truths."

Ever since I've committed myself to living an authentic life, I've enjoyed a rise in self-respect and a greater trust in my abilities. I now feel confident to share my thoughts and opinions with others, which has allowed me to form stronger and more genuine relationships. Knowing and being true to myself has made it easier to make major life choices and embrace the unknown. Being authentic has encouraged me to accept my strengths and weaknesses and hold myself to my own standards, as opposed to the standards of others. I have found peace in letting go of that which does not serve me well and I have come to realize that I'm pretty awesome. I'm living my life my way and it feels badass.

Life's Greatest Challenge

> ### Bossing Up in Action
>
> *Jack Kaladjian, CEO & Co-Founder of Park and Finch, Montreal, Canada*
>
> *"Knowing who you are is the cornerstone to developing your confidence. Overall, this helps you live to your fullest potential, allowing you to operate and execute at a higher degree. A confident person is smart, beautiful, happy, successful, positive, and is always pressing forward. Having confidence in who you are will allow you to create and conquer. Knowing who I am has empowered me to make the right decisions for myself and my business, without overthinking things. And my confidence has enabled me to achieve all that I'm pursuing. To help me stay true to myself, I spend 10-15 minutes a day connecting with my closest friends. I believe sticking to this routine is what keeps me grounded. If I could fast-forward 10 years and tell my future-self anything at all, it would be: remember who you are, stay humble and keep going."*

"It is not your responsibility to want the life that others want for you." - Colin Wright

Notes

Notes

Chapter 6
Ctrl Alt Del

Eliminating All That Does Not Serve You

Going through life is easy; growing through life takes effort. As a fellow Boss, you know that growth is fun, exciting, and necessary to succeed. But you also know that growing can be uncomfortable; they're called growing pains for a reason, after all. Remember puberty: that glorious period of your life when you were overly-emotional, totally self-absorbed, and your attitude had no chill? Eventually, you did learn that to be a respectable adult, you had to let go of certain thoughts, behaviors, and habits to allow new ones to develop. This is called "unlearning".

The process of unlearning is what psychologists call "proactive interference". Proactive interference occurs when your old ways inhibit you from fully adopting and maintaining new ones. This is based on **interference theory**, a theory of human memory that posits that learning and growth is compromised when past learned behaviors interact with newly introduced behaviors. This conflict negatively impacts growth.

One of the greatest obstacles in acquiring knowledge and in changing behaviors is the requisite disassembling of all that we've worked so hard to build, especially if what we're disassembling had once had any sort of successful track record. It isn't particularly challenging to learn new things when they fit comfortably within our worldview; but new things that challenge our view of the world is a different story. We grow very attached to our assumptions and expectations that were developed over time. We're conditioned to build upon what we know, and as a result, we have an adverse reaction to change. Nevertheless, to grow *is* to change, and it sometimes becomes necessary to risk the comfort of some of what we've learned in order to learn more.

Relying on outdated information is often the very obstacle that hinders us from achieving our goals. The world around us is evolving at such a rapid pace, and as people, we evolve along with it. It makes sense then that your ideas, perceptions and behaviors must also evolve in order for them to continue to serve you. You can't expect to elicit better results by using the same information and behaviors that you have always used. It just isn't possible (and remember, that is insanity). So, how can we eliminate old information that no longer serves us and make room for new information that will? We must *unlearn*.

Unlearning doesn't mean you must wipe your memory clean, Men-in-Black-style, in order to be successful. *All* learning is unlearning if you think about it: you're replacing old, powerless information with new, powerful knowledge. Unlearning frees up the space in your brain occupied by limiting thoughts and behaviors, and makes room for new learning opportunities. Consequently, unlearning paves new paths to success.

Without the weight of self-limiting beliefs, you'll be happier. When you're happier, you're more productive. Imagine how unstoppable you could be if you could unlearn the thoughts, beliefs, and behaviors that cause you stress, anxiety, and pain. Imagine the opportunities that would surface if you felt empowered, free, and calm. It will take effort, but it's possible to achieve. Here's how:

- Start to gain an awareness of repetitive thoughts, actions, and behaviors that don't contribute to your happiness and success.

- Recognize that which does not serve you well and eliminate it.

- Assess your wants and needs and establish new thoughts, actions, and behaviors that *do* contribute to your happiness and success. Take this opportunity to set your expectations and standards high... really though, shoot for the moon, this is your life we're talking about!

- Take initiative and learn something new. Your thoughts, actions, and behaviors are limited to what you know. Unlearning often requires you to acquire new skills. So, take a class, join a group, or read a book: interacting with other people and new sources of information challenges habits that are deeply rooted in our minds.

- Don't be hard on yourself if (read: *when*) you slip back into old habits. This will, however, slow or stunt your progress. It takes sixty-six days on average to form a new habit. So, be consistent and remain patient.

- Rinse and repeat. Check in with yourself regularly to make sure that your habits reflect your goals. If they don't, start back at the top.

Thoughts and ideas are shared, enhanced, and discarded regularly. We know this to be true of the outside world, yet we cling to what's in our minds as if it was sacred, even to the point of it holding us back. Those who are willing to question their assumptions are happier, adapt better to change, remain relevant, and achieve greater success. So, ask yourself, *what thoughts, behaviors, or habits should I unlearn in order to reach my full potential?*

Now ask yourself what you're waiting for.

"The illiterate of the 21st century will not be those that cannot read and write, but those who cannot learn, unlearn and relearn."

- Alvin Toffler

Notes

Chapter 7
There's Been a Change of Plans

It's Better to Bend Than to Break

I've moved more times than I have fingers... and toes. I've changed schools, changed friends, changed careers, changed life paths, and I've changed as a person. Needless to say, my plans have changed more than a few times. I'm okay with that, I like change. I'm happy when I'm in motion and I enjoy moving with the ebb and flow of life. That's often hard for people to understand. My lifestyle appears unconventional, when really, I just refuse to let it be rigid. Why? Because rigidity causes things to break.

We sometimes take for granted things that come naturally to us. Intrigued by the benefits of adaptability, I set out to understand how I learned to be flexible so that I could help others do the same. Ironically, I found an answer that really resonates with me in the business book, *The Platinum Rule*. In it, Tony Alessandra and Michael O'Connor suggest that adaptability is made up of two distinct components: flexibility and versatility. They explain that flexibility is a matter of attitude and *willingness* to change, whereas versatility is a matter of ability and *capability* to change. Fortunately, being capable of change can be learned and improved upon over time. Even if you aren't capable of making a change today, you *are* in control of your attitude. Making the conscious choice to be flexible in your ideas and expectations will positively influence your ability to change and adapt to unfamiliar situations.

Adaptability is essential in avoiding imposed success. It's often easier to take the path most travelled and go through life with a *"this is just how it's done"* mentality. But do you just want to *"do"* life, or do you want to maximize the time you have? You have seventy good years on this earth, eighty if you're lucky, to make the life you want and to get out of it what you can. Pursue your own version of success, take the path less travelled, get lost and discover entirely new routes. Life will put obstacles in your way, some that will seem unconquerable. Just begin with the willingness to try, and the capability will follow.

Even if the whole *"path less traveled"* thing isn't for you, adaptability is still a worthwhile area in which to invest your energy, both in your personal and professional life. Here's why:

Professional Adaptation

The professional landscape is changing. Old markets disappear, new markets emerge, audiences change, and the way you sell and market your product or service changes as well. Employers want and need workers who are adaptable to meet the demands of their ever-evolving organization. More and more, they are seeking people who are not stuck in their ways, who will embrace change, and who won't panic if things need to be rerouted mid-journey.

Whether you run your own company or work for someone else's, here are a few reasons why being flexible in the workplace contributes to your Bossing Up journey:

- If you're part of an organization that regularly undergoes changes, instead of getting frustrated, being able to easily adapt will help you to realize that there's no perfect system; we're all just trying our best to find our way.

- Every new skill, software program, and lesson you learn makes you even more valuable, whether it's within your current company or at your next opportunity.

- Being flexible often requires that you think on your feet and make something work out of nothing. Succeeding at this at work will help you feel more capable of taking on similar challenges in your personal life.

- Understanding different work styles and learning how to accommodate them will not only save you time and frustration, they will make you a better communicator.

- Your team counts on you to resist crumbling under pressure. Practicing agility, if only initially for them, will prove that you're stronger than you likely give yourself credit for.

Personal Adaptation

I speak with many people who commit themselves to a single path and then act as though they've backed themselves into a corner with no way out when things don't go as planned. If you embody only one lesson from this chapter, let it be this: **give yourself permission to change your mind**. Flexible people are happier people.

Being flexible will help you to successfully adjust your thoughts, behaviors, and expectations when things go unplanned, making it easier for you to pursue your desired direction. Here's what you can do in your everyday life to gradually increase your flexibility and improve your ability to adapt:

- Try changing your environments. If you work from your home office, try working from the living room or kitchen. Push through your initial discomfort.

- Practice staying calm when you *really* want to lose your shit. Maybe the cashier at the grocery store has rubbed you the wrong way. Count to ten, take deep breaths, or fantasize about reaching over the counter and getting hauled off by security. Do whatever you have to do internally to keep your cool.

- Don't put all your eggs in one basket by planning for a single outcome. Always have a backup plan, or at least think about what one might potentially look like, in case things go sideways.

- See the positives in all situations. Getting a flat tire while dropping your kids off at school sucks, but be grateful for the extra time you spent with them. Take the opportunity to help them practice for their spelling bee while you wait for roadside assistance.

- If it comes, let it. If it goes, let it. Go with the flow of things and try to embrace change. It's often in the winds of change that we find our true direction.

It's easy to get caught up in the moment and feel that once we've committed to something we must stick the landing, but it's so important to give yourself permission to change your mind. The path you chose six months ago may have been the right one for you to take at the time, but it doesn't mean it's still the right path for you to take today. Evolving is normal and exciting; with it, new insights, lessons, and opportunities arise that can and *should* influence your next steps.

However, you shouldn't only wait for new opportunities to present themselves to re-chart your course. If you don't like the path you're on, or if you don't feel fulfilled, change something. Sometimes you may only need to make a slight change in perception, other times may call for a complete life overhaul. Regardless of the magnitude of change you're seeking to make, it's important to remember that just because you started something, committed to someone, or thought, *"this is how it's meant to be,"* it's not enough reason for you to continue moving in that direction. You have to be happy. It has to be worthwhile. Practicing being flexible on a daily basis, if only in small ways, will better equip you to adapt to unforeseen changes and deliberately make ones that will get you one step closer to achieving your goals.

"It is not the strongest of the species that survives, nor the most intelligent, but the one most responsive to change."
- Leon C. Megginson

Notes

Notes

Chapter 8
Nah

Life's Too Short to Settle

If you're pursuing a life of imposed success, then you're settling. I hope that if you *are* settling, at least you're comfortable. My true hope, however, is that you're not settling at all. I don't want you to settle in your career, in your friendships, in your relationships, hell, I don't even want you to settle for the avocado that's not quite perfect for tonight's guac (don't even get me started on perfectly ripe avocados). But forget what *I* want. Do *you* want to settle for an *idea* of success and go through life feeling complacent rather than complete?

If you answered yes, it's probably time you put this book down and we part ways. How did you end up with this paperweight and get eight chapters in, anyway?

If you answered no, we should be friends. I like you! As your friend, I'm telling you that you deserve more. You deserve to be happy. You deserve to pursue your dreams with confidence. You deserve to achieve these dreams. You deserve to live a life that you're proud of, not one you've settled for.

Ditching Excuses Exercise

Pull all your excuses and justifications out of your head and put them onto paper or on the screen. Do any of them look like this?

- I really want to do it, but guess I don't really *need* to do it.

- If only I had more money, time, patience…
- Now is just not the right time.
- I suppose it's just not meant to be.
- I have so many things to be grateful for, why do I feel unfulfilled?
- This excitement probably won't last, I shouldn't waste my time.
- I could never do that.

When you can actually see your excuses, word for word, you can better face them. Whether the statements above are ones you're well acquainted with, or you have other self-limiting beliefs, you'll notice they're all self-justifying.

Don't ignore that inner voice. Don't try to silence what it's trying to tell you. Self-justification is your mind's way of defending its current position; if you feel the need to justify it, that's usually a good indication that you're settling. Remember, where you stand today doesn't have to be where you'll stand tomorrow. Like my ol' pal Jim Rohn says, "If you don't like where you are, move. You're not a tree."

You're stuck, not rooted. In order to get unstuck, you need to have a plan of action. Then you must *take* action. If you're not sure where to start, use these eleven steps to start building your plan:

1. **Identify something in your life that you're settling for.** Take an honest look at your environment, your habits, and the people you surround yourself with and ask, *If I could*

choose to be anywhere, doing anything, with anyone, would I be where I am now? If not, acknowledge what you would change. Is it your job? Your partner? Your health?

2. **Pinpoint what's limiting you and holding you back.** You might be saying to yourself, *I don't know what's holding me back.* If so, I'm calling bullshit. Remember, we're friends now, and friends keep friends accountable. You do know. Dig deeper.

3. **Assess if and how you've been blaming other people.** If the problem always seems to be other people getting in the way, there's a good chance it's *you* that's in your way. It's time to stop pointing the finger and start taking ownership of your situation.

4. **Recognize what it is you want instead.** If what you have isn't what you want, what do you want instead that would truly make you happy?

5. **Acknowledge what you'll need to do to make the change.** Do you need to lose weight? Earn more? Relocate? Think about what it would take to make a change and then think about what the first step would be to make it possible. It's important to start small so you don't get intimidated by the work ahead of you.

6. **Establish what's within your immediate power to change.** It's good to practice big-picture thinking, but if you don't focus on what you can do in the short term to help yourself get there, you'll forever be daunted and may not take the first step.

7. **Ask yourself if you *really* need those things to make the change.** If what you want and what you have are radically different, sometimes making major changes is necessary. However, oftentimes it's just an excuse. You may find that there's less in your way than you anticipate.

8. **Set REAL goals for yourself.** Once your desires have been screened for excuses, it's time to start setting goals that you'll actually stick to. More on REAL goals in Chapter 21.

9. **Make a list of who's in your support network.** Creating a list of people to lean on for support is a great exercise to remind yourself that you're not in this alone. Get your crew on speed dial and hit the call button when you need help or reassurance.

10. **Stop thinking and start doing.** Begin by changing what you can, today. Every ounce of progress is one bit away from settling, and one bit closer to fulfillment. Don't overthink your action plan, just start.

11. **Avoid thinking "it could be worse."** Sure, it could always be worse. But it could always be better, too. Always seek the positive in every situation by repositioning your thoughts from "what's the worst that can happen?" to "what's the best that can happen?"

In *Mistakes Were Made (But Not by Me)*, an exceptional book that focuses on justifying beliefs and choices, Social Psychologists Carol Tavris and Elliot Aronson dive deep into self-justification, owning up to the decisions we make, and holding onto delusional beliefs. They explain that not all self-justification is bad:

Self-justification has costs and benefits. By itself, it's not necessarily a bad thing. It lets us sleep at night. Without it, we would prolong the awful pangs of embarrassment. We would torture ourselves with regret over the road not taken or over how badly we navigated the road we did take. We would agonize in the aftermath of almost every decision: Did we do the right thing, marry the right person, buy the right house, choose the best car, enter the right career? Yet, mindless self-justification, like quicksand, can draw us deeper into disaster. It blocks our ability to even see our errors, let alone correct them. It distorts reality, keeps us from getting all the information we need and assessing issues clearly.

While settling isn't the same as making a mistake, there's something to be taken away from this concept of self-justification. If you're so caught up in justifying the choices that you've made that have left a void in your life, you're closing your mind to valuable information and emotions that can identify what's missing in your life and as well as to the know-how to achieve it.

"There is no passion to be found in settling for a life that is less than the one you are capable of living." - Nelson Mandela

Notes

Notes

Focus on Progress Instead of Perfection

Part 3: Focus on Progress Instead of Perfection

"When you obsess over every misstep or criticism, you become your own roadblock to growth." – Ariel Kaye

Shout-out to all my fellow perfectionists who just cringed reading that—I feel your pain! This is something I still occasionally struggle with. However, I know now that if I wait until something reaches perfection, it usually won't see the light of day. I also know now that when I've got my perfectionist goggles on, there's a whole world of hidden opportunity I miss out on because it's over there chillin' in my blind spot.

The relationship between perfectionism and success is a dangerous one. If you're one who wants things to be perfect, chances are, you also aim to be successful. And if you're anything like me, your (im)perfect brain works something like this:

- I'm going to start a business!

- This is going to be a GREAT adventure!

- I just need to get clear on the services I'm offering, get my website up and running, and set up a PayPal account. (You then create a mind map breaking down potential services, buy a domain name, set up a PayPal account, spend far too long choosing a website theme, and clear your schedule to start working on the greatness.)

- I have everything I need to get started, but ugh, my pictures are outdated and I really should also have a blog. Damn,

I'm not active on social media, I ought to get on it. (You do all that and are now 2 months behind.)

- Okay, *now* I'm ready…

- Wait, wait, wait. I just saw another site and that person had half the amount of text on it that I have. I should probably scrap everything I have and start writing all my text over from scratch. Yeah, that's what I'll do.

- Oh, and I definitely need an email marketing platform so I can share all my fabulous updates via my newsletter.

Then you realize that there will be no fabulous updates or registrants for your newsletter BECAUSE YOU HAVEN'T LAUNCHED.

If you're striving for perfection, at some point your enthusiasm will begin to fade, and you may convince yourself it's probably better to not start at all than to start something imperfect. In other words, you're stuck—and you're not going to get unstuck by chasing something that doesn't exist.

So instead of being imprisoned by perfection, break free by focusing on progress instead. I know it sounds crazy, but there's nothing stopping you from making adjustments along the way and enhancements as you go. Keep success within reach and make the process more enjoyable by shifting to a progressive mindset. A progressive mindset focuses on the journey, not the destination. It sees setbacks as lessons rather than failures. It encourages you to celebrate your wins, regardless of how big or small they might be, and motivates you to get across the finish line. This does not mean that you shouldn't set the bar high. Set that bar as high as it will go. But give yourself some wiggle room, and allow for imperfection.

The following chapters will serve as your guide to stay focused on progress and kick your perfectionist habits to the curb.

Notes

Chapter 9
Words Not to Live By

Abandoning Self-Sabotaging Thoughts

Oh, self-sabotage. You know, the thoughts that create a bullshit story that reframe your aspirations and keep your goals just out of reach. The ones that keep you in an infinite loop of mediocrity, blocking you from reaching your full potential, and keeping you in a state of stuckness... yeah, those. Why do you do that to yourself? I'm willing to bet that if you spoke to others the way you speak to yourself, you'd be put into the loonie bin, or you'd get shot. Nobody would take that crap from you. Why are you taking that crap from yourself?

Before you start self-sabotaging over your self-sabotaging ways, let's get something straight: there's nothing wrong with you. The part of your brain that prevents you from reaching your goals is the same part that serves as a safety mechanism that protects you against disappointment. When there's a risk of getting hurt, your brain thinks it's doing you a favor by keeping you comfortable, and it tells you your big dreams aren't achievable or worthwhile. Twisted! But we know success won't be found in the familiar quarters of your comfort zone; you've got to step outside the box. Doing so will allow you to take back the power from your self-limiting beliefs, and make more progress.

You'll never sabotage yourself into a person you love. Escape your cycle of negativity by stopping negative self-talk in its tracks, discerning thoughts from facts, and identifying a solution, as follows:

Thought: I'm not going to get any work done for my thesis today because I've got a full day of meetings ahead, then I've got to pick my daughter up from school, cook dinner, give her a bath, and I will be exhausted by the time I put her to bed.

Fact: Today will be bananas. It's going to be a challenge to work on my thesis, but surely, I can find thirty minutes to make even a little bit of progress.

Solution: I'm going to use my commute to work to flesh out some of my half-baked ideas so that I can have a starting point to revisit tomorrow.

Whether you think you can or you think you can't, you're right. Success is a matter of mindset, which is entirely within your control. Self-empowering thoughts take the same amount of brainpower as self-sabotaging ones. So, why not give self-empowerment a shot for once? A happy brain results in a happy life. If you're like me and you have an aversion to fluff, that statement might make your eyes roll, but it's true. Experiencing a state of happiness stimulates your brain and encourages it to respond in a way that reinforces pleasure. By doing things that make you happy making yourself happy, you're actually training your brain to keep you happy.

Ditching self-sabotaging thoughts and trading them for self-empowering ones not only makes you more enjoyable to be around, it increases your ability to enjoy life. Now, this isn't about believing the world is all rainbows and unicorns, but I urge you to understand the psychological and physiological effects of self-empowering thoughts so that it will compel you to flip the switch on the crap you tell yourself. That stuff weighs you down... ain't nobody got time for that.

A happy brain:

- Increases your awareness of your environment, which positively impacts your interactions with it
- Reinforces existing neural connections and stimulates the growth of new ones
- Improves your ability to acquire and process knowledge by increasing mental productivity
- Enhances your capacity to analyze and think objectively
- Increases your level of attentiveness
- Leads to more self-empowering thoughts and behaviors

In a commencement address by Jim Carrey to the students of Maharishi University of Management, he shared:

"You can spend your whole life imagining ghosts, worrying about the pathway to the future, but all there will ever be is what's happening here and the decisions we make in this moment, which are based on either love or fear. So many of us choose our path out of fear disguised as practicality. What we really want seems impossibly out of reach and ridiculous to expect, so we never dare to ask the universe for it."

Focus on curating self-empowering thoughts and dare to believe in positive possibilities. Here are a few ways to train your brain to think happy:

Think about how you can improve yourself. Pinpoint areas of your life that you feel are limiting your growth and focus on improving one area at a time so that you can approach them more effectively. Ask those you trust for their opinions on what needs improvement; keep an open mind and embrace vulnerability. You won't regret it.

Stop, drop and roll. Make a conscious effort to stop what you're doing throughout the day, if only for a few seconds, and check in with yourself. Drop whatever thoughts and behaviors are working against you and let the good vibes roll.

Have fun. It's so easy to get caught up in the daily grind and feel that there's just not enough time in our day for enjoyment. Do something just for fun, be a little silly, embrace any opportunity to smile and laugh, particularly when you're stressed. This will reset your brain and fuel it with the endorphins you need to push yourself forward.

Do something you're good at every day. Tap into those skills that you haven't made time for lately. Perhaps you're a great chef or basketball player? Doing those things that make you feel good and that you excel at reminds you to enjoy life, encourages you to more frequently do what you're good at, and empowers you to take control of your happiness.

Make time for your health. Take thirty minutes a day and spend it on healthy choices, whether that's exercising, prepping food for the week, or meditating. Making your health a priority makes you happier, prolongs your life, and helps you to reduce stress and manage it more effectively. Diminishing stress also diminishes the opportunities for self-sabotaging thoughts to creep in.

Surround yourself with positivity. It's hard to stay in a self-sabotaging headspace when you're surrounded by positivity. Declutter your home, bring fresh flowers or your favorite action figure to work, and spend more time with those friends who make you feel good and who are positive themselves. Small efforts every day will make a big difference in crushing your self-limiting beliefs.

Practice positive self-talk. Remember to stop negative self-sabotaging thoughts in their track. Assess the situation and come at it with solutions rather than with frustration. Turn your kindness inward and treat yourself the way you treat others. Tell yourself that you are strong, you are capable, and you *will* accomplish what you set out to accomplish whether or not you are fully and immediately convinced.

Sure, these are handy tips, but if you don't implement them, they'll be of no value to you. You've got to do the work. Write these down, save them in your phone, get it tattooed on your forearm, I don't care, but keep them close because knowledge isn't power until it's applied.

Self-Sabotaging vs.	**Self-Empowering**
I've never done anything like this; I'm probably going to fail.	This is a great opportunity to learn something new; I may even discover a hidden talent.
It's just so complicated; I'm completely overwhelmed.	I need to take things one step at a time and raise my hand when I need help.
I could do it if only I had more _____, but I don't, so I can't.	I know resources are seldom the issue; what can I do to be more resourceful?
I'm too busy.	So I won't be able to get to it this week; how can I prioritize my responsibilities to fit it in next week?
I'm clearly not good at explaining things to others.	Everyone learns differently. I'll pay closer attention to how my team works and seek a more effective approach to communicate with them.
I'm not getting any better.	Practice makes perfect.
It's too risky.	I'm going to take a chance on myself.
I'm not good enough.	I deserve this and am absolutely worthy.

You won't obliterate all self-sabotaging thoughts and behaviors overnight, but by making a consistently conscious effort, your self-powering thoughts will take precedence and you'll become less critical of yourself and your surroundings. Consistency is key here. It may feel unnatural, silly, or useless at first, but it does pay off. At the end of the day, you need to be your own biggest cheerleader because if you don't think you're worthy or capable, no one else will.

"You gotta own up to your limiting beliefs and self-sabotaging habits so you can disown them." - Karen Salmansohn

Notes

Notes

Chapter 10
~~Tomorrow~~

The Time Is Now

There's a very real disconnect between much of what we're taught as children and what it takes to be a successful adult. From as far back as I can remember, I was taught to wait. Wait for the bus, wait in line, wait for my turn, wait for my snack, wait for the bell. As a kid, I learned that good things come to those who wait. As an adult, I've learned that good things come to those who decide to go for it. Waiting for instructions slows you down or stops you from advancing altogether, and before you know it, life will have passed you by.

Full disclosure: I don't particularly buy into the "there's never a right time" mentality. Some times are better than others, and it helps to be aware of various circumstances when making that call. Let's say, for example, you've gone above and beyond what's required at work, you've continuously exceeded your boss' expectations, and you feel that your current salary no longer reflects your new responsibilities. You finally get the courage to ask for a raise. You walk into your boss' office guns blazing, ready to begin the monologue that you've been practising all week, and you learn that she had just put her dog down earlier that morning.

WARNING: Holster those babies real quick. Now is **not** the right time.

There is a difference, however, between acknowledging that now is not the best time to take action, and making excuses to avoid taking action. The latter, let's face it, is more often the case. You may think that if you don't start, you can't fail. This is indeed a great way to avoid a fear of failure, but a terrible way to live a fulfilling life. Maybe you'll take action *when*… you have more energy, you lose weight, you find the one, you're back on your feet, you retire, you're dead? *When* affirmations keep you stuck. Why? Because they, too, are self-sabotaging thoughts: by telling yourself that you don't have what it takes to act *now*, you have in effect thrown in the towel before you have even begun. In those moments of self-doubt, procrastination, and laziness, there will never be a right time. There probably will never even be a good time, and if there is, you'll likely be too uninspired to seize it. Or, it may sneak by unnoticed altogether.

Later turns into tomorrow, tomorrow turns into next week, next week turns into next year and next year never comes. NEWS FLASH—progress isn't made when you're waiting—to start your diet on Monday, to make more money, to find the one—it's made when you start making moves. Stop waiting for the "right time" and start doing things *right now*. Put the chocolate bar down, start your passion project, create a Tinder profile. Do whatever it takes to get the ball rolling.

Everything you could possibly need to become successful is within arm's reach. Now is the time to stop questioning yourself, to believe in your potential, and to step into your power. Don't be sucked in by the false promise of tomorrow. The only thing that's guaranteed is today.

~~Tomorrow~~

The longer you find reasons (read: excuses) to avoid taking action, the less time you have available to take the plunge. Your happiness and success aren't waiting for you in the future, nor have they passed you by. They're right here, waiting for you to create them, *right now.*

"The desire to start something at "the right time" is usually just a justification for delay. In almost every case, the best time to start is now." - Gretchen Rubin

Notes

Notes

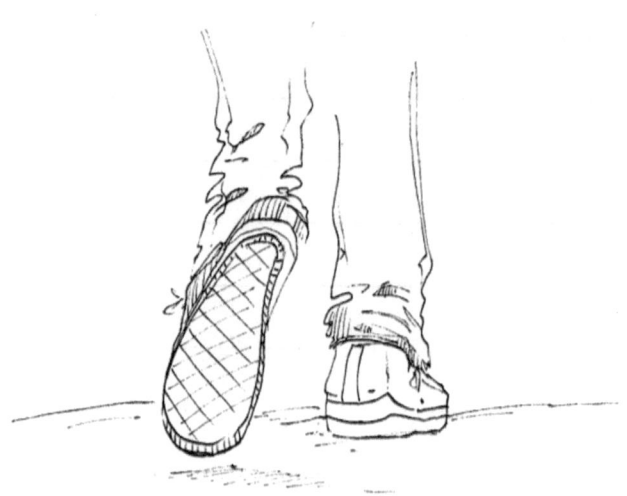

Chapter 11
Usain Walked Before Usain Bolt

Start by Taking the First Step First

When I started my business, I was under the impression that I could hit the ground running and turn a profit in no time. I wasn't delusional, I was *confident*, but I was also wrong. I had big goals, elaborate plans, and I was ready to conquer the world. I set my sights too high, too soon, and I was relying on a wobbly ladder made of hopes and conviction to get me to the top. I didn't necessarily think my new venture would be easy, but I was naively unaware of just how much I had to learn, and just how many repairs my trusted ladder would require. I had grown so used to achieving success in the corporate world so quickly that when my new success came at a much slower pace, I felt discouraged. I had fallen into the trench of despair, tripped by instant gratification.

Isn't it crazy that we can send a picture in real-time to our best friends overseas, transfer rent to our landlords in seconds, and order dinner from an app and have it waiting for us when we get home? When everything we could ever imagine is no more than a click away, it's mind-blowing to be reminded that some things take time. We may eventually be able to hit "update" and download certain skill sets, but until we're no longer human, the truth is, "running" takes effort and time. According to Malcolm Gladwell, author of the best seller *Outliers*, it takes 10,000 hours to become a master of any skill.

While you may not have 417 days to dedicate to becoming an expert at *something*, surely you can acknowledge that success takes practice and patience. If your goal is to lose weight, whether you want to lose five pounds or fifty pounds, you've got to start by losing the first pound. If your goal is to get over your fear of swimming, you'd be better off by exploring shallow waters first, rather than jumping straight into the deep end. If your dream job became available, it would be a good idea to give your resume a facelift and write a wicked cover letter before opening the door for dialogue. The point is, whatever your goals are, you need to start somewhere.

It was a tough pill for me to swallow, but when I came to terms with the fact that it would take time to build a successful business, my perception changed. I no longer felt discouraged. I realized that starting my own business was an entirely different race from that of the corporate world. I embraced the start-up life, but I had an ongoing curiosity about how I was going to scale my company. Every conversation, every case study, and every article led me to the same simple conclusion: think big, act small. Everyone from solopreneurs to some of the world's biggest brands credit their success to setting ambitious goals and taking one small step at a time.

Google's former Senior Vice President of Adwords and AdSense, Susan Wojcicki, discussed some of the principles that keeps Google ahead of the pack:

"No matter how ambitious the plan, you have to roll up your sleeves and start somewhere. Google Books, which has brought the content of millions of books online, was an idea that our Founder, Larry Page, had for a long time. People thought it was too crazy even to try, but

he went ahead and bought a scanner and hooked it up in his office. He began scanning pages, timed how long it took with a metronome, ran the numbers and realized it would be possible to bring the world's books online. Today, our Book Search index contains over 10 million books."

Many of us have big aspirations and want to get there at lightning speed. We aim for too-much, too-soon, without fully realizing the small steps needed to get there. This was very much my reality in the early stages of my business. Inspired by the idea of Larry Page scanning pages of books at home, I began to adopt this way of thinking and have since applied it to both my personal and professional goals. Starting small has allowed me to *comfortably* step outside my comfort zone, prove concepts, and gain confidence in my ability to succeed at something new. With one eye on execution and the other eye on the bigger picture, I'm better able to plan my next step and foresee where I might need help, allowing me to appropriately prepare myself for when I get there. Here are some ways you can apply thinking big and acting small to your goals and start making immediate progress:

Prioritize longevity. Success is a marathon, not a sprint. In order for "think big, act small" to be effective, the two need to go hand-in-hand. Thinking big can stifle productivity if you feel the urgency to do it all right now. Breaking it down into smaller, achievable tasks will help you set a healthy and realistic pace that will make it easier to maintain your stamina and enthusiasm.

Test the waters. Think about what you want to achieve, what's driving your goals, and how you define success. You may realize there could be multiple ways to reach your goals. Instead of overthinking every possible outcome, and eventually talking yourself out of even trying, test different approaches to find one that feels good.

Examine your role models. Don't break your head over trying to reinvent the wheel. Look at those people and companies you trust and respect, and figure out how they've been able to succeed. Learn what worked for them and replicate it according to your goals, values, and environment.

Anyone can put together a complex plan, but if complexity is all you see when you start, you'll drown in a beautiful pile of post-its, multiple Excel sheets, and presentations that will never see the light of day. It takes finesse to manage a complex plan. Starting small is the key to success.

> *"A journey of a thousand miles begins with a single step." - Lao Tzu*

Notes

Chapter 12
Wing It

To Be Honest, I'm Totally Winging It. My Life,
My Eyeliner, My Everything.

I like structure. It keeps me focused. But I consciously resist being confined by it because I've learned that no matter how much I plan, stress, or overthink things, some things will always be beyond my control (it pains me to write it, but it's true). My stepfather always says, "You want to make God laugh? Tell him your plans." This is his way of saying life has a tendency of throwing curveballs when you least expect it—and he's right.

As you've likely experienced, these curveballs can turn out either for better or for worse, but rarely as you would expect. When you're fixated on your plan, unfavorable curveballs can result in feelings of anger, frustration, or anxiety. Winging it enables you to accept whatever life hands you, rather than trying to mould life exactly to your expectations and winding up disappointed. And winging it certainly comes in handy when focusing on progress instead of perfection.

I work with a brilliant man who is notorious for perfectly timed and seamlessly delivered idioms. One of my favorites is, "Sometimes you just have to build the plane mid-flight." This dramatic example of the need for improvisation resonated with me so strongly the first time I heard it because it's basically my life philosophy. There's currently no big end-goal for me, nor is there a final destination. I have ambitious goals, and there are certainly things I'd like to experience on my life journey, but I admit I don't know where I'm going—there's no grand finale plan. I'd argue none of us really know where we're going; but I'll digress from that for now. The point is, my route is ever-changing, and there are times when the engine craps out, and I've got to do whatever it takes to remain airborne.

There's one incredible example of building a plane mid-flight that's just too good not to mention. It's the story of Sir Richard Branson's brainchild, Virgin Airlines. Stuck in a Puerto Rican airport, Branson was among a group of people waiting to fly to the British Virgin Islands. There weren't enough passengers to make the trip worthwhile for the airline, so the flight was cancelled. Instead of moping around or getting angry, Branson devised a plan to fly to the British Virgin Islands, and he recognized a potential business opportunity in the process. He scouted around the airport with a blackboard that read '$39 one way to BVI', approached everyone who was waiting, and ultimately sold enough tickets to charter a plane. Off he went …what a guy.

For *you*, building a plane mid-flight might mean transitioning your hobby into a business. It might mean that you finish your slide deck *only after* sufficient people have registered for your webinar. Or, perhaps it means juggling all the moving pieces after a tough break up while staying on top of your game at work. Improvisation will help sway you with the ebbs and flows of life.

Here's how I wing it in the heat of the moment:

- **Acknowledge when you're getting frustrated.** You're allowed to feel frustrated, but try not to let it consume you. Take a moment to truly understand what's bothering you, try and find the silver lining and attempt to reframe your situation positively.

- **Remind yourself everything will be okay.** Life can be tough, and sometimes it gives us more than we think we can bear. Rest assured, whatever is happening, it's not the end of the world. Unless you've woken up to a zombie apocalypse—then you're screwed.

- **Embrace the five-second rule.** No, not the rule for eating food off the floor. I'm referring to the rule that encourages you to count backwards from five to one when you have an impulse to act on a goal. This rule urges you to physically move within five seconds to avoid your brain killing the idea. Get out of bed, turn on your computer, grab your car keys, take any action to move you one step closer to achieving your goal.

- **Woosah (breathe).** Proper breathing powerfully affects every system in your body, particularly your nervous system. When you're faced with something unexpected, good or bad, take a deep breath to center yourself. If you feel stressed, adopt an incremental breathing pattern by breaking your inhalations and exhalations into four parts. Inhale to 25 percent capacity; hold. Inhale to 50 percent capacity; hold. Inhale to 75 percent; hold. Inhale to 100 percent; hold. Exhale in the same fashion. Repeat until you begin to calm down.

- **Laugh it off.** On average, children laugh 200 times a day, whereas adults only laugh twenty-six times. Aside from the physiological effects of laughter (lowered blood pressure, reduced stress hormones and muscle tension), laughing also helps us to keep things in a positive perspective. We take ourselves far too seriously. Laughing helps you to enjoy the good times and to reframe your mind so that you can more easily cope with the harder times.

Keeping cool when you're in the heat of the moment is most effective when you practice winging it regularly. Just like in sports, you need to train off-field so you can be at your best at game time. Although "winging it" suggests an attitude of going with the flow, there are things you can do to help guide the flow. This is how I practice:

Recognize that you can't control everything. We all know this basic truth, yet we still fight it… but maybe I'm projecting. All the structure, planning, spreadsheets, and wishful thinking in the world won't enable you to control everything. Accept that there will indeed be unexpected happenings that were unaccounted for in your plans; be willing to take them as they come and reroute as needed. Resistance will only get you stuck.

Give yourself kudos. It's important to give credit where credit is due, especially to yourself. Acknowledge times when you're not fazed by an unexpected change and reward yourself for being able to go with the flow. This positive reinforcement trains your brain to keep at it.

Deliberately change your routine. The more you challenge your comfort levels on your own terms, the easier you'll be able to roll with the punches when something happens beyond your control. Take a different route to work, leave your bed unmade in the morning, do something that you don't really want to do that has little to no impact on your life. This proves to yourself that you don't need to be so rigid.

Say yes. Have you ever noticed that we're often inclined to say no? Even when we want something, we tell ourselves no. When we need help, we say, *"No thanks"*. This keeps us in a subconsciously closed-off state. It's no wonder we freak out at the unexpected: we're so used to being in our bubble. Say yes to the plans you want to make, say yes to accepting help, and say yes to new opportunities. Yes is a small word that makes big things possible. Say it often.

Meditate. Sports psychologist and mindful meditation teacher, George Mumford, is credited for stepping up the game of NBA titans, Michael Jordan, Shaquille O'Neal, Kobe Bryant and more. He teaches them that mindfulness is more about being in the flow than going with the flow, although both offer similar benefits. He says, "Meditation is not trying to go anywhere or do anything, meditation and being present is just seeing what's there and letting it speak to you. The goal is to be present to what is." Being present can help you observe your surroundings without being affected by them, which is a great skill to have when faced with something unanticipated.

Trust yourself, release your inhibitions, and know that no matter what, things will be okay. You *are* going to weather a few storms, some more severe than others, but just because your engine failed doesn't mean your plane is going down.

> *"Everyone is winging it, some just do it more confidently."* - Pamela Druckerman

Notes

Notes

Chapter 13
You Can't Multitask

But You Can Master the Micro Moments

Many of us wear the "multitasker" label as a badge of honor and we convince ourselves that we're good at it. However, several studies have shown that multitasking can impair your cognitive control. We tend to think that we're superheroes, efficiently managing our time when we're simultaneously attending a meeting, engaging in a group chat, and typing an email. In reality, we're not multitasking; we're just shifting our focus from one thing to another very quickly (and I mean really fast, sometimes it takes just a tenth of a second)... and while that may sound like a superpower, it actually weakens our brains.

Contrary to popular belief, our brains can only focus on one thing at a time. If you think about it, each time we engage in a secondary or tertiary task, we aren't really doing them at the same time at all. There's a start/stop/start process that goes on in our brains: start the text message, stop the message, start the email. The real kicker is that rather than *saving* us time, multitasking often *costs* time because we end up being less efficient and making more mistakes. Being busy doesn't equate to being productive.

The long-term effects of training our brain to jump from task to task include difficulty organizing our thoughts and trouble paying attention and recalling information. Nobody *wants* to contribute to any of these problems, but if they don't cause immediate consequences, they're dismissed as future problems and are filed in the "*I'll deal with that later*" folder in our brains—similar to global warming, which gives me serious heartburn, guys! WE NEED TO SAVE OUR PLANET. But back to the point, there *are* immediate effects to "multitasking". When we multitask, we risk making silly mistakes such as sending a text message to your boss instead of to your mom (I've done that, and yes, it was embarrassing), or sneaking the wrong word into an email that has nothing to do with what you're writing about and everything to do with the cooking show that you're watching while writing. We're also generally less aware when trying to do multiple things at once. For example, most of us can simultaneously drive a car and listen to a friend talk, or to music. However, I'm willing to bet that you can recall yourself having once driven through an unfamiliar part of town, and slowed down, turned down the music, or stopped responding to your friend on the phone. It's kind of weird because neither music nor talking impacts your vision, right?

Here's where it gets interesting. In a study about being on a call while driving, Steven Yantis, a professor in the Department of Psychological and Brain Sciences at Johns Hopkins University, shared:

Directing attention to listening effectively 'turns down the volume' on input to the visual parts of the brain. The evidence we have right now strongly suggests that attention is strictly limited—a zero-sum game. When attention is deployed to one modality—say, in this case, talking on a cell phone—it necessarily extracts a cost on another modality—in this case, the visual task of driving.

MRIs have been taken to see how much of the brain is activated while driving in silence versus how much is activated once listening is layered on. They revealed that the amount of attention spent on driving decreased by about 37 percent.

A 2012 study by David Strayer, a Professor of Psychology at the University of Utah, determined that multitasking *is* possible, but only for the elite 2 percent of the population with the superpower to do so without losing efficiency. The good news is that for the rest of us 98 percent who lack this wicked awesome gift, there's still hope. Life doesn't stop because you're busy, and being *efficient* rather than attempting to multitask will help you make progress.

Efficiency is all about "mastering the micro moments," a term I picked up in the tech world, where a digital company's viability is contingent upon the ability to make critical decisions in as little as ten milliseconds. While I don't have billions of dollars riding on my decisions (yet), and my brain will possibly never process information that fast, I've developed a new appreciation for time and how to get the most done with the time I've been given.

Here's how I use my time efficiently and make progress on my goals:

Prioritize. Yes, the floors need vacuuming and the dishes need doing, but they can wait. Separate the "would be nice to do's" from the "must do's" and rank the latter in order of importance each day.

Schedule time for the important tasks as if they were important meetings. This is something I'm notorious for. About 40–50 percent of my calendar is time I've booked with myself to work on certain projects. I've learned to respect my time as I do my clients' time, which has helped me to ensure that important things don't get pushed around and ignored throughout the week.

Reassess the time spent on tasks. Have you ever booked an hour-long meeting with someone only for the meeting to be cut unexpectedly to a half hour? Chances are you were still able to get the information you needed to take the next step. Reassessing what tasks need to be completed and how much time they should realistically take can save you time, ultimately making more time for other things.

Have a plan (and stick to it). Whether it's for your day, a project, or a pitch, making a plan and going in prepared will allow you to be more efficient. Planning is also helpful in making you feel confident in your ability to execute. Imagine that you had multiple errands to run in different parts of the city: if you don't consider travel time, traffic hours, and proximity to each errand stop, you would waste a lot of time commuting, rather than getting stuff done. Simply put, you can accomplish a lot with a plan.

Factor in some "reactive" time. There will always be things that occur during the day that you didn't plan for and which will require your attention. Set aside time each day to allow you to react to the unexpected so that you're not panicked to address these surprises in between tasks.

Don't schedule every minute of your day. It's important to give yourself some downtime in a day. Not only will taking a minute to recharge increase your productivity, your brain could face difficulty integrating information and solving problems if it's overworked. If an opportunity comes up for you to go outside, do some mid-day squats, or just people-watch from a cafe, take it. If it doesn't, create the opportunity yourself.

Delegate. Time is wasted and productivity is lost when you take on more than you can handle. One of the fundamental tips to making progress is to delegate tasks to others who can perform them better than you. Delegating enables you to power through the things that play to your strengths while eliminating tasks that are potential blockers for you.

Communicate. Poor communication results in lost time and patience. A quick, half-hearted email (likely written while multitasking) with little regard for detail can end up adding many unnecessary hours to a project. Effective communication is beneficial for many reasons, but it's particularly helpful when delegating. It's a good practice to think through your objectives and how to articulate them in order to achieve your desired outcome. It may require some additional time at the beginning, but it can actually shave days from a project.

Find hidden pockets of time. This is somewhat of a multitasking hack. Hidden pockets of time are everywhere, you just have to know where to look. They allow you to make the most of your time in limbo. Unlike downtime, I refer to limbo as the time spent doing monotonous tasks that are not particularly exhilarating, but need to be done nevertheless. You know the times when you feel like there are *so* many better things you could be doing? With some awareness, being stuck in limbo can help you cross several things off your to-do list at once, without needing to worry much if they were done well. For example, I'll water my plants while brushing my teeth, I'll check my voicemail while I'm walking my dogs, and I'll do my online banking while I'm on hold with the insurance company. Time is rarely wasted when you know how to optimize it.

Eliminate distractions. Book a meeting room for yourself, turn the music off, put your phone away, delete Facebook (temporarily—don't freak out!), pack your lunch, put noise-cancelling headphones on—help yourself to stay focused by being aware of what distracts you and eliminate or mitigate these distractions to the best of your ability.

Better yet . . .

- **Go MIA.** I find great benefit in going off the grid, whether hibernating for a weekend and completely extricated myself from work or going away for a week and detaching myself from all devices and responsibilities in order to focus on myself. Either way, taking a little time to focus on what needs to be done goes a long way.

- **Seek balance.** Identify areas of your life where there's an imbalance of effects. Acknowledge how much of your input is generating the best results—whether that's happiness, time, money, etc.—and find ways to make those efforts a priority and reduce or phase out those that don't serve you.

You Can't Multitask

You have 1,440 minutes in a day. What you spend them on has a direct impact on your ability to achieve success. Leave yourself notes, set your alarm as a reminder, alter your routine, but whatever you do, make your time work for you by focussing on what's going to move the needle forward.

"There is nothing so useless as doing efficiently that which should not be done at all." - Peter Drucker

Notes

Notes

Chapter 14
Treat Yo'self

Forget What Ya Heard, It's Okay to Be Selfish

Success isn't just a matter of achieving your goals, it's also about enjoying the process. Crossing things off your checklist will not make you feel successful if you don't get pleasure from it. Doing things that you *want* to do is just as important as doing what you need to do. If you don't pepper in some fun, your motivation will start to dwindle.

How often do you do something for yourself? Not for your partner, your child, or your team, but for *you*. A little dose of selfishness is a key ingredient to the secret sauce of success. There, I said it! "Selfish" is a notoriously dirty word, loaded with guilt and fear of judgement, but it doesn't need to be. Reframing the importance of making yourself a priority will encourage you to do more of what makes you happy, without remorse—and remember, happiness and success go hand in hand. They're like peanut butter and jelly, butter and popcorn, or milk and cookies. Great, now I'm hungry. The point is, don't put this one off. This isn't one for the *"I'll deal with this in the AM"* pile. Let's do a happiness health check together right now. Ask yourself these questions and answer each one honestly before moving onto the next one.

Happiness Health Check

☐ Do I care about my own happiness?
☐ Does my health and happiness come second to others?

- ☐ Has my happiness been compromised?
- ☐ When did I last do something for myself? *Having a cup of tea or taking a shower* **does not** *count.*
- ☐ Am I looking forward to anything that I'll be doing for myself today?
- ☐ Is there more I could do to make time for myself?
- ☐ Am I making enough of an effort to do things that make me happy?
- ☐ Do I feel guilty when I put myself first?
- ☐ Do I wait until my bladder is about to burst before taking a bathroom break because I'm *always* needed somewhere or by someone?

We're not even making time to pee, people!

Although we know the importance of being happy, we easily get stuck in a constant loop of justification that looks something like this:

- People depend on me, if I don't take care of this no one else will.
- It's not *so* bad.
- I chose this, now I have to live with it.
- I just don't have time to do the things I want to do.
- I really shouldn't be focusing on myself right now.

I get it, trust me, I really do. But you do know what will inevitably end that loop? A burnout. And what good will you be to yourself and those who rely on you if you become miserable or ill? Contrary to what you may have tricked yourself into believing, putting yourself first is *not* the same as disregarding everyone else's needs.

It's easy to ignore ourselves when we're constantly pleasing others. We tell ourselves that caring for others is what life's all about; that our self-contentedness is driven by their happiness; that if they're happy, we're happy. While that may certainly contribute to your happiness, if that's what you're relying on to fill your happiness bucket, it will never be full and you'll become exhausted trying to fill it. It can't be all about them all the time. You've got to make your happiness a priority.

Taking Back Your Happiness

There are several ways to put yourself first every day. Let's do another exercise, shall we? This is one that Emily Williams, founder of I Heart My Life, does with her clients and one that I've integrated into my practice as well.

Think of five activities that make you happy and make a list of them. Here's mine, in no particular order:

1. Networking with like-minded people
2. Travelling for pleasure, as opposed to work (though I like travelling for work, too)
3. Trying something new (a new dish, activity, etc.)
4. Movie night in with my boyfriend
5. Exercising

Now think about the last time you did those activities. For me:

1. Networking with like-minded people (two weeks ago)
2. Travelling for pleasure (nine months ago)
3. Trying something new (two weeks ago)
4. Movie night in with my boyfriend (two nights ago)
5. Exercising (two days ago)

Check your second list to see if anything has been neglected recently, or if you haven't done something as recently as you'd have liked. From my list, I can identify two areas that need improvement. I aim to have no more than one consecutive rest day in my fitness routine, so, I need to pick up the slack there. And it also looks like I'm due for a vacation (opens tab #thirteen to start looking up deals), hooray! The truth is, I too have put vacation off because I've convinced myself that my clients need me, that this isn't a good time to take off and that I should be spending the money elsewhere. But honestly, there's nothing that a little planning can't solve. And when I think back to my last vacation, I realize that—surprise, surprise—no one died when they didn't hear from me within minutes (RUDE).

While I find it very gratifying to contribute to other peoples' happiness, the minute I begin to feel that I'm losing myself, or that a situation isn't contributing to my own happiness or growth, I know it's time to make a change, or to just walk away. When I make such decisions, it's not because I've given up: it's because I trust myself, and I know that I need to continue to make myself happy to keep that trust strong.

It took me many years before I started putting myself first, but I can tell you with confidence that it has made a world of difference. Making time for me and my needs has positively impacted my relationships, my health, and my business.

We are by-products of our relationships. We are friends, parents, children, colleagues; we are driven by the relationships in our lives. Yet our relationships are often the first to suffer when stress levels rise. Putting myself first has allowed me to keep a pulse on my own wants and needs which keeps me present. The more present I've been, the better my relationships have become. I'm mindful of others' needs, but I'm not consumed by pleasing them, and am always conscious to not neglect myself. Knowing and liking who I am outside of my relationships has led to better, more genuine connections.

Putting others first kept me often on the run. I got up early, got in late, and often ate on the road. This resulted in a lack of sleep, not enough time for my personal projects, and an unhealthy diet consisting of whatever I could grab to eat at the gas station. Needless to say, my physical and mental health suffered. I have since taken control of my health. I may wake up just as early, but my priority now is exercising. I'm up just as late, but I have made time for hobbies and down time. And I have made a greater effort to plan ahead and pack snacks and meals that better accommodate my nomadic lifestyle. These changes have made me happier; I have more patience, I feel better, I'm more alert, and I'm more capable of getting more accomplished in a day (I didn't even know that was possible).

I was a "yes" woman when I started my business. I bent over backwards to accommodate any and all client requests in order to minimize the risk of losing their business. My clients began to expect too much of me, and it was no fault of their own; I agreed to everything and anything, no matter how ludicrous the request, how unrealistic the expectations, or how much a miracle it would take to pull it off. I did it all with a smile on my face, while quickly losing steam behind the scenes. I needed to embrace no because I simply did not have the capacity (whether mentally, or time-wise) to deliver. Respecting my limits and putting myself first allowed me to properly manage expectations, and relieve myself of the burdensome feeling of saying yes all the time. Putting myself first has allowed me to perform better and exceed my clients' expectations.

If you think you can't afford to take the time and money needed to take care of yourself, the reality is, you can't afford not to. Working yourself into the ground is not an option. Why? Because being dead is bad for business. Putting yourself first means prioritizing yourself on your agenda; you can't solely focus on prioritizing your tasks. So, call an old friend, go for a run, or hit the journal: it's the little things after all that go a long way toward building a fulfilling, happy life.

A happy mind is a progressive mind. So, go ahead, treat yo'self.

"When you treat yourself right, you run better and more efficiently. Which means you don't have to go 100 miles an hour to get everything done." - Ann Curry

Notes

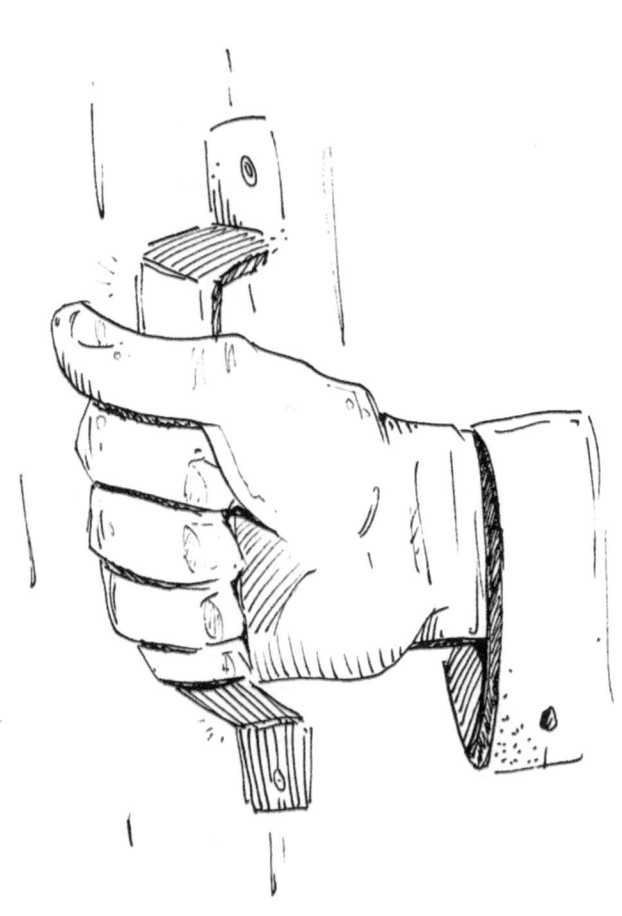

Chapter 15
Doors Are for Opening

Something a Wise Homeless Man Taught Me

It's so important to take "you" time. To stay healthy and happy, it's imperative to get into the habit of making yourself a priority and keeping your best interests at the forefront of your mind. But that doesn't mean keeping people in your shadow. A big part of Bossing Up is empowerment: it's about learning, evolving, building the best version of yourself, and then sharing that goodness with others. Success doesn't come from constantly being in your own bubble, concerned only about your own goals and status. Success comes from implementing change, and change can't happen in isolation.

When I was about eight, I remember going to the movie theater with my dad. A homeless man opened the door for us in the hopes of scoring some change. My dad gave me a few coins to toss into the man's cup and thanked him for holding the door. The homeless man responded, "If you're not opening doors for people, you're closing them." That has stayed with me ever since.

Why do we hold doors open for people, anyway? Maybe we are consciously thinking of doing something nice, maybe we were taught it's the polite thing to do, or maybe it's just habit. Whatever your motive, it all comes down to the same thing: we want to make it easier for the person behind us. It's our subtle way of saying, 'Hey, life is tough enough as it is, let me help you out."

P.S.: If you don't hold doors open for people, stop being a jerk. Your mama raised you better than that.

In life, we encounter many closed doors. Some are meant to remain closed, others are just not ready to open, and some require a little help. Opening doors for others, or keeping them open can completely change the course of someone's day, career, or even life. In business, however, it's easy to fall prey to the dog-eat-dog mentality. Introductions are often very transactional and new connections are only seen as potential favors and titles, rather than as human beings. Opening doors is the equivalent of extending opportunities, which is an extremely powerful success strategy that often goes overlooked, or is deliberately ignored.

Opportunity makers attract and achieve success far more easily than opportunity hoarders. Being an opportunity maker goes beyond offering wealth, knowledge, or contacts. It's the willingness to take pause and to help others to realign and readjust themselves so that they're better positioned to succeed. It's the capacity to blend your talents together to accomplish more than you could on your own. It's the ability to communicate with the intention of connecting over a shared interest, and putting the proper pieces in place to turn an idea into action.

When you step away from self-serving motives and adopt the mindset of an opportunity maker, you'll experience a quantum shift in perspective. You'll start to see beyond your bubble and you'll be exposed to new ideas and possibilities all within reach. You become invested in the happiness and success of others, which leads to a greater happiness and success of your own.

Suddenly, you'll realize that you're no longer alone on an island—you have a community that can bring you to new heights. That all starts by offering to help.

The following are my twelve golden rules for opening doors and creating opportunities for others. They have made a real difference in the lives of my peers, colleagues, and clients, and have significantly impacted my personal and professional growth. Although you may practice some of them already, ask yourself how you can enhance your efforts.

- **Initiate communication.** Fear blocks opportunity and may very well be the reason someone won't approach you. Eliminate fear from the equation by making eye contact, smiling, introducing yourself, or making small talk. But take the initiative to get the conversation rolling.

- **Pay attention.** When you pay attention to what someone is telling you as well as to what you're telling them, you're benefitting everyone. Your words, your expressions, and your body language should indicate that you're present in the moment and want to be an active contributor to the conversation.

- **Make genuine connections.** When's the last time you left a networking event feeling like you *really* got to know someone? Step outside the norm, learn what others are passionate about, ask about past experiences and current business needs. Allow yourself to be somewhat vulnerable, and share your story and aspirations. Getting to the good stuff allows you to jump into opportunity maker-mode early in the relationship.

- **Take notes.** Whether it's in a meeting, on a business card, or in your phone, make a note of others' goals and expertise so that you know what kind of tool you're adding to your tool belt.

- **Be open-minded.** You're not going to like and agree with everyone, and that's okay. You'll meet people who challenge your thoughts and beliefs. Try expanding your horizon and seeing the world through their lens.

- **Encourage others.** Acknowledge and praise others when they've shared something with you or when you've recognized an accomplishment of theirs. Help them leverage their strengths and encourage them to continue moving forward.

- **Ask how you can help (and deliver).** You may have an idea that would bring value to their life, but you're not a mind reader. Straight up ask what you can do for them, and if it's something within your power, do it. Trustworthiness paired with relevant, unrivaled value will keep you top of mind for future opportunities.

- **Connect people.** Share the wealth of your resources, but be mindful of who you are connecting. You'll want to ensure that your network remains strong, and that means introducing people who will be of equal value to each other.

- **Give generously.** As you know, we must often rely on friends, family, and peers to get an idea off the ground. So, buy their book, offer your knowledge, download their app, share their resume, eat at their restaurant, like their

Facebook page: just do what you can. A small gesture goes a long way, and will always come back to you in some form.

- **Give credit where it's due.** Nobody likes an attention hog. Keeping the credit to yourself stifles collaboration, reduces innovation, and limits growth. You're better off sporting the reputation of a trustworthy team player than the reputation of an accomplished, but credit-hoarding solo player.

- **Be on the lookout.** Opportunities won't always come knocking at your door, you need to regularly seek them out. Attend events, join online groups, and reach out to people beyond your network. Be on the lookout for yourself as well as for those who you want to help to elevate.

- **Follow up.** Make a habit of sending an "it was nice to meet you" email, add new connections on appropriate social media platforms, or go the old-fashioned route and give them a call. Relationships need to be nurtured. Even when there are no opportunities yet to be made, stay in touch to let them know they're a valued member of your network and that you're still around to help if needed.

Opening doors for others has become part of my DNA, and consequently, much of my success has been driven by the help of the very people for whom I held the door open. I'm basically a professional door (wo)man... I should put that on LinkedIn. Seriously though, adding value to other people's lives has never taken any value from my own, it has only contributed to it. I've learned and I continue to learn so much about myself and what drives my happiness when I give without expecting anything in return. The people with whom I've connected have become my biggest advocates and have largely contributed not only to my success, but to who I am today.

"The doors we open and close each day decide the lives we live."
- Flora Whittemore

Notes

Chapter 16
So, You're a Hot Mess

The Trick to Not Sweating the Small Stuff

"Don't sweat the small stuff," they say. We've heard it a million times, yet we're *still* sweating. We get tripped up over the little things and eventually we get stuck. How you allocate your energy is crucial to getting unstuck and making progress. It's all too easy to fall down the rabbit hole of getting worked up with no way back to the surface. One of the biggest lessons in my journey has been to acknowledge what's actually deserving of my time and attention. So much of my energy has been given to the little things that frustrated me rather than motivated me. Spoiler alert: those things were never the ones that moved the ball forward. Letting go of the things that needlessly drained my positivity and productivity was, and continues to be, one of the greatest gifts I've given myself. It doesn't come without practice though. These are the tools I use to not allow myself to go crazy over the small stuff:

- **Remember you're not in control.** We tend to think that the more control we have over things, the happier we'll be: then off we go on our quest to control everything in our power, whether consciously or subconsciously. However, when we fail to rule the world, which inevitably will happen, we feel unhappy, anxious, and worried. While this concern may spark a necessary fire under your ass in certain scenarios, when you're in a situation over which you have no control, worrying is ineffective and will stunt your progress. Loosen your grip and acknowledge that things will play their course, and that regardless of the outcome, you *will* be okay. Chances are you won't care about what you're stressing about this time next month, anyway. Save your energy for what matters.

- **There are very few emergencies.** Unless you're a doctor or you're saving lives in another capacity, there are very few things that need to be dealt with RIGHT NOW. Yet, we have grown accustomed to living in a very hurried state. As a result, we over-dramatize deadlines and impose needless stress on ourselves. I'm definitely a repeat offender on this one, but when I catch myself doing this, I remind myself that most things, especially the small stuff, don't require immediate attention.

- **Stop complaining.** Complaining isn't productive; it will keep you stuck. It takes more time and energy to complain about something than it does to think about a solution. When things don't go your way (and this will happen because, remember, you're *not in control*), take the opportunity to reroute or change directions altogether. Everything, I mean everything, is a learning opportunity. You may have to dig a little deeper to find it sometimes, but I assure you, the lesson is there. As Dennis P. Kimbro, Ph.D. says, "Life is 10 **percent** of what happens to us and 90 **percent** how we react to it." Stop complaining and find something to be happy about.

- **Don't let bad days happen.** You know those days ... the days when everything annoys you from the moment you wake up. You're stuck in traffic, you spill your coffee on your shirt on the way to work, and the spawn of Satan is sitting behind you on the bus. But this isn't a bad day. Why? Because there's actually no such thing as a bad day *in reality*. A bad day only exists *in our interpretation* of reality. Sure, the scenario above is an awful way to start the day, but it doesn't mean the rest of the day will be a write-off. However, the moment that you believe that the rest of the day is for naught, you've inevitably committed to flushing it down the drain. I like to think of those shitty moments as speed bumps rather than stop signs. While they may slow me down, I refuse to let them bring my day to a complete halt.

- **Appreciate the little things.** Just as there are little things that can derail your mood, there are little things that can enhance it as well. Enjoy the moment and appreciate the sun on your face, or take the time to thank your colleagues for their help on getting a project over the finish line. It will boost your happiness and productivity.

- **Recover quickly.** I've worked with companies whose mottos have been "fail fast" or "fail forward." This is supposed to encourage their team to try new things, assess whether the decision was a good one, and if not, kill it fast before spending additional resources. And above all, learn from the mistake. While I share the sentiment that mistakes are important for learning, I think these companies have only got it half-right. The word "fail" is negative and demoralizing; that's not how you or your team wants to feel. The intention is to learn and to maintain optimism for the next task. So, make the mistakes necessary for learning, recover as quickly and with as little loss as possible, and don't sweat it—mistakes are a vital part of the process.

- **Pick your battles.** Conflict is a healthy part of all relationships, both personal and professional. Whether it's with your parent, partner, or boss, it's important to assess if the battle can be won and if it's worth fighting for. I start that assessment by asking myself, "Is what I'm upset about actually the problem, or is there something else that's bothering me?"

I've been able to avoid conflict on several occasions by realizing that the other person usually has very little to do with what I'm upset about. If you've reflected and still feel there's an unresolved issue that you need to address, I suggest you identify your ideal outcome before having that conversation. Being solution-focused helps you keep your emotions at bay, and it encourages the person you're engaging with to embrace change, rather than their fears and insecurities. With this process, it's important to consider whether your ideal outcome is fair to everyone involved, so, ideally, everyone can leave feeling it's a win-win.

- **You can't please everyone.** As a recovering people pleaser, I know this one is hard, but the sooner you accept it, the happier you'll be. You'll notice there's a lot less small stuff to sweat over when you come to terms with the facts:

    a. You can't make everyone happy.

    b. Not everyone is going to like you, and that's okay.

    c. You deserve to say no to things you don't want to do.

- **Have an open mind.** We're more prone to getting worked up when we're on the defensive, and we typically get defensive when we feel insecure or threatened. You'll become more confident and less bothered by the little things by keeping an open mind instead, and by learning how to deal with negativity and criticism effectively.

Attention to detail, or, to the little things, can be beneficial in the prevention of mistakes, in planning ahead, and in being efficient. It's definitely a contributing factor to your success, but a fixation on details can be detrimental. Overthinking a bunch of little things clouds your vision, making it nearly impossible to make progress. This is another kind of getting stuck that behavioral specialists call "analysis paralysis." Oftentimes, the little things you're obsessing about either have little to no impact on the big picture.

Sweating the small stuff can make you feel like you're losing your marbles. Your thoughts go around in circles, you feel like you're not getting anywhere, and anxiety and self-doubt kick in. These negative emotions consume brain space and leave less working memory to tackle the bigger, more rewarding tasks, causing your productivity to plummet even further. It's extremely difficult to remain creative, ambitious, and optimistic in this state.

Keep your eyes on the prize, whatever that may be for you, and practice not sweating the small stuff as part of your daily routine. You'll notice over time, as the saying goes, that it is indeed *all* small stuff. And when you're not stressing and over-analyzing every—single—thing, life becomes more enjoyable.

You may just find there's very little distance between you and the success you seek.

"To live a good life: We have the potential for it. If we can learn to be indifferent to what makes no difference." - Marcus Aurelius

Notes

Chapter 17
Why Are You Bringin' Up Old Shit?

Letting Go of Failure

We've all "failed" at something, and yet here we all are. We all survived, we bounced back, and some of us can even laugh about it. But it's still something we fear deeply. Interestingly, what scares most people is failing to do something right the first time. This fear is the flipside of the pursuit-of-success coin for many. It's immobilizing, often prohibiting us from seeking what we want, and it's entirely unrealistic. We can't really expect ourselves, or anyone else for that matter, to do anything right the first time around. But we do. Why?

When you consider how any person—even you— or any company has grown, it all boils down to trial and error. We all fell after taking our first steps, dated a few bad eggs before recognizing what we want in a true partner, or made some poor investments before becoming financially secure. We know this to be true, yet we continue to have a hard time embracing any trial period because we fear making an error. "Error" just doesn't sound nice. No one *wants* to be wrong or make a mistake, but I firmly believe that's where the disconnect occurs and where fear seeps in: all errors are lessons. They're not so scary when you consider them as such. When you alter your perception, you'll notice that these lessons are usually not harmful, but often helpful and necessary. I'd push to change the term "trial and error", but "trial and learnings" just doesn't have the same ring to it. In moments of doubt, try to believe— and I mean *really* believe—that you won't ever know what really works for you without knowing what doesn't. It's through the learning process that you'll improve upon your trials, and ultimately succeed.

Psychotherapist and author, Tina Gilbertson, identifies family values as one of the sources from which this fear frequently stems. In her book *Constructive Wallowing: How to Beat Bad Feelings by Letting Yourself Have Them*, she encourages her clients and readers to reflect on their family values in order to understand better the friction failure creates. She explains that they can create internal conflict in the following ways:

- Humility: *You think you're all that? You should be ashamed of yourself.*

- Security: *A bird in the hand is worth two in the bush.*

- Having it all together: *If you don't know what you're doing, don't bother.*

- Being selfless: *If you fail, you'll have wasted precious resources on yourself.*

- Not taking more than your share: *You should be happy with what you've got.*

- Hard work: *If you fail, it's because you didn't work hard enough.*

- Perfection: *You only get one shot at this. You'd better get it right!*

I don't know about you, but I always find it so fascinating and somewhat reassuring to learn that self-limiting beliefs, on some level, have been learned—and can therefore be *unlearned*.

I guess this is as good a time as any to confess that I have a slight obsession with the fear of failure. It is, without a doubt, the ultimate cause of stuckness for many of the people I know and work with. The idea of failing triggers negative emotions such as disappointment, sadness, confusion, frustration, anger, and regret. While these emotions are unpleasant, they are not in and of themselves what people most fear: the culprit of this ugly fear is *shame*.

Guy Winch, PhD and author of *Emotional First Aid: Healing Rejection, Guilt, Failure*, explains:

"Shame is a psychologically toxic emotion because instead of feeling bad about our actions (guilt) or our efforts (regret), shame makes us feel bad about who we are. Shame gets to the core of our egos, our identities, our self-esteem, and our feelings of emotional well-being. The damaging nature of shame makes it urgent for those who have a fear of failure to avoid the psychological threats associated with failing by finding unconscious ways to mitigate the implications of a potential failure."

I remember having an "Aha!" moment when I first read that. It really puts fear of failure into perspective. Basically, our brains are trying to do us a favor by protecting us from shaming the very core of our being. Yikes, that's deep. Our brains trick us into thinking we'll inevitably and irrevocably fail, and then ultimately, we begin to believe that we'll never succeed and often abandon our goals mid-journey or choose not to begin at all. By better understanding this process, we can begin to fix the problem. And let's face it, even though our brains mean well, this *is* still very much a problem.

What Worked for Me:

I don't remember being afraid of failure as a child, and I can't quite pinpoint when or why that changed, but throughout college and university, I didn't want to do anything that I thought I wouldn't be good at for fear of looking stupid. I took myself far too seriously and closed the door on several fun opportunities and great experiences. That all changed when I learned about the different ways that companies strategize for success. I took the tools from my favorite model, SOAR, and began to plan for my most preferred future. The confidence I felt in my plan made me feel more secure in my ability to execute, and, over time, it allowed me to let go of my fear of failure and feelings of shame.

The acronym 'SOAR' stands for:

Strengths: acknowledge and own what you do well

Opportunities: consider what may have an impact on your efforts

Aspirations: identify your goals

Results: determine what will be

If you're familiar with strategic planning analyses, you have probably heard of SWOT, which is more common and stands for strengths, weaknesses, opportunities, and threats. I much prefer SOAR, particularly for personal development. Although "strengths" and "opportunities" are retained from the SWOT model, the SOAR approach adds the critical process of appreciative intent by including the elements "aspirations" and "results." Thinking about your aspirations and results enforces a more positive mindset after all, unlike SWOT, which puts a heavier emphasis on weaknesses and threats. SOAR helps you to build your plans on a platform of that which works, rather than on a platform of trying to fix what doesn't. Weaknesses, threats, and ultimately failure are not ignored in SOAR, they're simply reframed and given the appropriate focus within the opportunities and results conversations. "Reframed" is the key word here, Bosses. If you haven't noticed yet, perception is a recurring theme in this book, and will largely shape the way you make progress and succeed, or don't.

You don't necessarily need such a model to help you conquer your fear of failure, but I've found this extremely helpful when embarking on new or major projects. Another simple but effective action you may take to conquer fear is to tell others when fear is keeping you stuck. Fear of failure is something we typically keep under wraps; God forbid someone should know you're afraid. But speaking aloud about your fear will help you come to terms with it. It's also quite a liberating feeling to let it out of your head and into the world; confronting your fear makes it a little less powerful than it was yesterday before you spoke about it. Sharing your fears with those you trust typically results in garnering reassurance, and the boost in morale they can offer will often encourage you to take action.

When facing your fears, it's a good time to revisit "think big, act small." This mentality is especially helpful when facing your fear of failure, as it encourages you to (re)gain your confidence by taking baby steps and making little bursts of progress. For example, if you've "failed" to turn your hobby into a business because you "just don't have time", set a small goal to move steadily forward: take fifteen minutes today to think about the different ways you can make money; fifteen minutes tomorrow to research how you can accept payment; and fifteen minutes the next day to start thinking about the content you want to have on your site. Act small, act regularly.

Letting go of fear is an ongoing process. With practice, it will alleviate the pressure of perfection and make room for progress. Throughout this process, it's important to remember that if at first you don't achieve the results you want, that doesn't mean you've failed. It means you have more to learn. There's no error, there's no failure... there's only learning.

"There is freedom waiting for you,

On the breezes of the sky,

And you ask "What if I fall?"

Oh but my darling,

What if you fly?"

— *Erin Hanson*

Notes

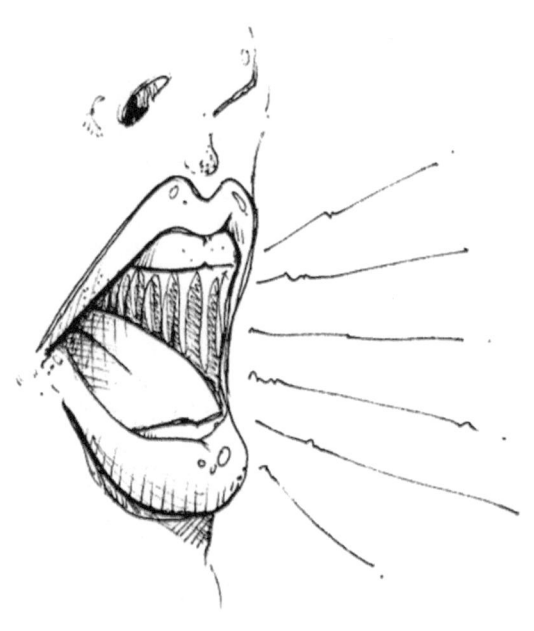

Chapter 18
Google Doesn't Always Have the Answers You Need

Asking for Help IRL

In the corporate world, I had no problem asking for help. I knew that my team was stronger together than we were alone. Together, we made progress faster, we felt more empowered, and we reached our end goal every time. Something changed as I entered entrepreneurship: I was so disillusioned by the glory of running my own business that I wasn't prepared for the plethora of help I would need, and I convinced myself somewhere along the way that I didn't *need* help.

I've always been stubborn and independent, but it never got in the way of raising my hand and asking for help, until it was *my* business that needed help. I didn't want to inconvenience anyone, and therefore I struggled without asking for any help for far too long. I thought that to be successful, I needed to take on the world alone. I didn't want to look weak or needy, so, I powered through every challenge, but the more I took on, the less productive I became. I quickly found myself in a sink or swim situation and I had no choice but to ask for help to enable my business to survive, much less succeed. It was awkward and uncomfortable at first, but the more I asked, the more I saw how eager people were to share their knowledge and expertise.

I was reminded that there were skills, experiences, and resources I needed, but didn't have. So, I started a Facebook group called Service Swap, which encouraged members to barter their skills and services in effort to help each other grow. There was so much talent within my immediate network alone that when they started inviting their friends and connections to join, the group truly became a force to be reckoned with.

Service Swap organically became a community of Boss-minded people, and has since evolved into the Bossing Up Members Area. Everyone in the group brings incredible passion, expertise, and support. If a question is asked and the members don't have an answer, they'll tag someone who does. As such, the group continues to flourish. You should put this book down and join the group right now. I guarantee you'll find someone who can help you start, grow, or enhance your project or next big idea.

The best part about the community is its ingenuity. It's a safe place for members to feel free from judgement for not having it all figured out. When someone says, "Let me know if there's anything I can do to help," they mean it. Members don't have to worry about being needy or imposing, because it's a platform created specifically to ask questions, collaborate on projects, and shamelessly promote the kick-ass things you're working on. As Janine Garner, author of *From Me to We* says, "When we support other people to be more successful, we discover opportunities for collaboration that ultimately enable us to be more successful ourselves."

Fast forward to today, with the support of my peers, asking for help has become the foundation of my success, and I surprisingly love doing it. I probably spend more time Googling than I do anything else, but certain things require human intervention. When I feel stuck, want advice, or just need to talk to someone who gets it, nothing compares to the guidance I'm given by my network. I've grown comfortable with asking for help by following these four techniques:

- **Think of whose help would make the biggest impact on what you're doing.** If you're going to ask for help, it might as well be from those people who can bring the most value to the table. Evaluate who this might be by assessing a list of people who've already offered help, and who know what you're trying to achieve.

- **Identify the kind of help you need.** Maybe you need help to finally assemble that shelving unit that's been in the box in your garage for months. Or, perhaps someone you know has a connection that you think would be valuable to promote your new business venture. Knowing exactly what you're asking for helps to cut straight to the chase without weird and unnecessary small talk. I mean, do be polite and ask how their day is going, or how their family is, but there's no need to catch up on life just to eventually get to, "*So anyway, I've got this thing I'm working on, and I was wondering if you could help.*" Such small talk diminishes the genuineness of your conversation, and it could make you seem like a bit of a shark.

- **Think about what you can do in return.** Revisit past conversations and try to remember if there was anything your contact was working on that you could help with. If nothing comes to mind, be sure to offer your help when you reach out. This is a tried and true method. Every single person to whom I've offered help in return for helping me has come through on my request, whether they helped me personally or introduced me to someone who could. A 100 percent success rate ain't bad! Offering my help has become an integral part of all new interactions. It sets the tone for collaboration and speeds up the process. I love growing my tribe and I appreciate when people take a similar approach.

- **Come full circle on the ask.** It's important to frame your request for help properly. Instead of sounding desperate or defeated by saying something like, *"I really need help, and nobody's helping me"* or *"Obviously I'm too stupid to figure this out on my own, can you help me?"* —take all the positive thinking you've been doing and put it into the ask. Be specific and make sure it's mutually beneficial.

Better ways to ask for help would be:

"Ken, I loved the presentation you did at the last workshop. Might you be able to help me with an upcoming presentation? I want it to be just as captivating. I'd love to help you with marketing the fundraiser you're working on in return."

Or:

"Alyssa, I've been following your design work for the last little while. I'm looking to get my logo redesigned, and think you're the best person for the job. Let me know if you're interested and what your rate would be."

Or:

"Lee, I've been presented with a really exciting project to work with some of the city's leading artists, but there's just too much for one person to do. It would be great to get you on board and it would be awesome for your portfolio. Do you want to go for coffee to see if this is something that we can collaborate on?"

For best results, make sure you express to your contact your appreciation of the value of their time and expertise, and that you have carefully considered what they stand to gain by helping you.

Bossing Up in Action

Thierry Lindor, Founder & President REMAX Griffintown and Influence Orbis, Montreal, Canada

I recently got a Facebook friend request from a man named Thierry. I didn't know him, but my hustle radar went wild after seeing his profile and who our mutual friends were. I knew he was someone I wanted in the Bossing Up family so I accepted his request. As a testament to how effective offering and asking for help can be, here's a peek at our very first interaction.

Me: *Hey Thierry, nice of you to connect. I hope you're having a great weekend.*

Thierry: *Hi Samantha, how nice of you! I'm having a busy weekend ... in my business, busy is good, so, I can't complain. What about yourself? How was your Saturday?*

Me: *Busy is good, indeed! I hosted a great networking event last night as a soft launch for my book release, so, it's been busy on my end as well. I'm in full beast mode to get the book across the finish line.*

Thierry: *Nice! What's the name of the book and where can I get it?*

> **Me:** *That's kind of you, thank you! The book is called Bossing Up; it's a personal development meets business book. It's a tactical guide for success based on the steps I took to get five promotions in five years, double my salary in the process, and take the leap to start my own business. I'll keep you posted with where you can find it once it's out. How about you? How can I help support you in your endeavors?*
>
> **Thierry:** *Great, well count me in! I'll definitely be a buyer and reader of your story! It's funny you asked that last part, Samantha, because one of my favorite phrases that has helped me win since I've been an entrepreneur and wealth creator has been: "How can I contribute to your ongoing success?" I'm working on something big and shall let you know very shortly how you can positively influence and contribute to my endeavors!*

This conversation was short, sweet, and entirely effective. In less than five minutes, Thierry acknowledged that I could potentially bring value to what he's working on. He introduced himself and started a friendly conversation, got right to the point, and asked how he could help support me, and he let me know he'd be reaching out for help in the near future.

The something "big" Thierry was working on was an incredible event for influencers, by influencers. I'm not talking about the elite Instagrammers of the world, I mean people who are influencing real change in their community. I had the pleasure of becoming an ambassador for the event and see some of the behind the scenes magic that made it happen. I learned that in order to make this dream a reality, Thierry sold his house, the land he bought for his future house and his car to self-finance the project. Now that's commitment! Without asking for help, his project could not have been the success it was. The first event was such a hit that he plans on taking the concept to Toronto, Vancouver, Paris and Casa Blanca.

Asking for help and accepting it has allowed me to accomplish so much more than I could have ever done on my own, but it required a shift in thinking to change how I was acting. As an early entrepreneur, I was what is called a Lone Leader: someone who believes that asking for help makes them vulnerable and less capable. The risk of looking weak prevented me from being open to receive help, much less ask for it. I had to retrain my brain to accept that help isn't a crutch to success, it's the elevator that gets me to the top.

What helped me to improve asking for help, as with anything in life, was practice. I began proactively asking for and accepting help in my personal life. I made a list of things I'd been putting off because I couldn't do them alone, and I wrote down who I could ask for help to get them done. As it turned out, there were a lot of things I was letting go undone because I didn't want to ask for help, and to my surprise, there were several people I identified as potential helpers. This small exercise was more valuable than I expected it to be. It allowed me to identify two important things. Firstly, I'm not in this alone. I know several people who would be more than willing to help me, but I had to ask. I had my "everything's under control" façade on, so people stopped offering their help, not because they didn't want to help me, but because I wouldn't accept it. Getting their support would mean allowing myself to be vulnerable, and while that felt uncomfortable, it felt better than being stuck. Secondly, procrastination comes in all forms.

I wouldn't consider myself a procrastinator. I'm a "get shit done" kind of woman, I'm making moves and progressing every day… I couldn't possibly be a procrastinator. But when I saw the list of things I wasn't getting to (read: putting off), it became clear that procrastination had seeped through the cracks of my foundation and I wasn't even aware of it. Having typed out onscreen all that I needed help with, I was forced to face all that I'd let drag on. While there were quite a few things on the list, looking at it suddenly didn't seem so daunting. When I stripped the hype away from what needed to be done, I almost felt silly for having put it all off for so long. Again, I reminded myself that feeling silly is better than feeling stuck.

I began asking for help with the little things, like changing a lightbulb that I couldn't reach because I didn't have a ladder, and for help watching my dogs on evenings when meetings ran late. I got help to finally put together my computer chair that I'd put aside in frustration and let sit in the corner until it collected dust. I also got help learning what to look for and what to ask when purchasing a new car. Starting small enabled me to become more comfortable with seeking help from others, and their support empowered me to ask for help for my business. I've asked for legal help, for assistance with building proposals, and for advice on how to handle certain situations. Certain things require the input of others who are more experienced or with different expertise than I have if I want them done properly.

Sooner or later, you too will realize that you don't have to do it alone; nor should you. The next time you need a hand, remember this: people want to help. Reciprocity and inclusiveness make people feel good. People's motivation to help is what psychologists call "prosocial behavior". The behavior of offering and accepting help leads to more consistent positive action for everyone involved. It makes us feel more connected to each other, and it reinforces a growth mindset for everyone involved, helping us all to win

"You can do anything, but not everything." – David Allen

Notes

Google Doesn't Always Have the Answers You Need

Notes

Part 4: Make Yourself Big

"Your playing small does not serve the world. There is nothing enlightened about shrinking so that other people will not feel insecure around you. We are all meant to shine, as children do. It is not just in some of us; it is in everyone, and as we let our light shine, we unconsciously give others permission to do the same. As we are liberated from our fear, our presence automatically liberates others."
- Marianne Williamson

Do you remember climbing to the top of the jungle gym, yelling, "I'm the King of the castle"? Do you remember having ambition so great that you wanted to be a veterinarian *and* an astronaut? Do you remember being the one at summer camp who got all the badges? If you've carried that passion and confidence into adulthood, kudos. Many of us lost that spark as we were growing up, and we have convinced ourselves that the drive we felt then wasn't real; we were *"just kids"*.

As kids, our families and our teachers tell us not to boast about our accomplishments because it's not nice and it makes others feel badly; that lesson continues to be reinforced as we grow up by society and our employers. Rarely were we taught that it's okay to embrace our confidence, or shown how to use it to fuel our dreams and encourage others to follow theirs.

So, somewhere along the way we stopped exuding our pride, we became wary of talking about our accomplishments, and we compromised ourselves, our ideas, and our goals to avoid offending or undermining others; humility that's been twisted into humiliation doesn't do anyone any good. Making yourself small does not mean someone else will feel big.

It's time to take back your pride and share it! I'm not talking about making self-aggrandizing statements, I'm talking about feeling excitement for your hard-earned accomplishments. It's important to validate yourself, because sometimes you're the only one who will do it. So, give yourself a much-deserved pat on the back and share your wins, whether it's a small one like finally organizing your desk, or a big one like closing a long-time-coming deal with a new client.

You can own your awesomeness without it being at the expense of others' egos. NFL Hall of Fame quarterback, Johnny Unitas, says, "There is a difference between conceit and confidence." And your confidence will indeed serve the world.

Notes

Notes

Chapter 19
Make It 'til You Make It

Because There Ain't No 'Fake' in the Hustle

Think back to a time when you had thought to yourself, *I'm just going to have to fake it 'til I make it*, and to your surprise, it worked! Now ask yourself, *Did I actually fake it, or did I just make it happen?* In most circumstances, I'd bet it was the latter. Maybe you forced a smile when you weren't really feeling it to intentionally try and lift your mood, and then found yourself feeling better. Maybe you struck a powerful pose before a presentation to boost your confidence, and then found yourself immediately empowered. Or, maybe, after being promoted to a role with requirements beyond your skill set, you consciously set out to act as your mentor would have, and then found yourself achieving success in the new position. The reality is: you're not *faking it*, you're *making* it happen.

"Faking it" is a load of shit because nobody likes a faker. But even more so, it's just not good practice. Faking it lulls you into a false sense of security that can often mask the real work that needs to be put in day in, day out, to achieve success. This is true for your relationships, your career, and everything in-between. Faking it can prevent you from asking questions that may benefit your endeavors because you're *faking* knowing the answers. Consider how that may cause you to miss opportunities. Appearing confident doesn't mean you feel confident anyway. The emotional labor it takes to fake the appearance of confidence while internally aspiring to feel confident will inevitably take a toll on you in the long run. And if at any point in your journey, you are revealed to be less than you claim to be, your credibility will take a major hit. By its very nature, faking it is dishonest, so even with the best of intentions, you'll still feel like a fraud.

"Making it," on the other hand, requires you to think creatively, use the skills and resources you possess already, and advance yourself. It's about being authentic. It's about taking the time to identify the person you want to be and working toward that version of yourself. As Harvard professor and best-selling author, Amy Cuddy, puts it, "Do it enough until you actually become it." Even so, as we're *doing it*, and making it happen, we may still feel like imposters.

Kicking Impostor Syndrome to the Curb

Perhaps you're familiar with the delightful thoughts that accompany Impostor Syndrome. You know, when you feel like a fraud. Well, you're in good company. Author Neil Gaiman shares, "The first problem of any kind of even limited success is the unshakable conviction that you are getting away with something, and that any moment now they will discover you." Maya Angelou also relates, "I have written eleven books, but each time I think, uh oh, they're going to find out now. I've run a game on everybody, and they're going to find me out."

You've got to laugh at the irony of the situation: those who suffer from Impostor Syndrome are actually trying to do good in the world; those who coast and don't seek to create value rarely become victims. So, if Impostor Syndrome resonates with you, then give yourself a good ol' pat on the back, because you're one of the good ones. Doesn't that feel great? (I hope you detected my sarcasm.)

Here are ten points to keep in mind when you feel as if the town has rallied with their pitchforks and are coming to do you some damage:

1. You're not alone; we're all just trying to figure it out.
2. Accept that you did/do/are doing something right to deserve this newfound opportunity.
3. Acknowledge that if what you're doing provides value, you aren't a fraud.
4. Scroll through tweets, Facebook messages, blog comments, and emails from people who believe in you to remind you what you're doing it for.
5. Learning and adjusting as you go *does not* make you a fraud—it makes you human.
6. Your skills can potentially change someone's world or even the world as a whole. By holding them back, you're not only doing yourself a disservice, you're also doing a disservice to others.
7. Don't succumb to being a fraud; if you don't yet have the answers, be honest about it.
8. Someone with fancy credentials doesn't necessarily know more than you.
9. Connect with someone who's going through similar impostor symptoms.
10. Putting yourself forth with honesty and transparency eliminates any potentially ill-time revelations about yourself.

When I first started coaching, I struggled with feeling like an impostor as well. I thought, *I can't just call myself a coach. I'm not certified. I've never coached anyone. I can't charge for this; that would be fraud!* In need of guidance, I jumped on a discovery call with my-now-business coach. With her help, in just one short hour, I came to realize:

I'm not just "calling myself a coach." I have been consulting companies for many years. By definition, a consultant is a professional who provides expert advice, which was exactly what I was seeking to do.

No, I don't have certification from an online institute that *claims* to be the LEADER in certified coach training. Nor do I have a fancy badge to put on my website that proves I paid for said training. But I do have three degrees and a decade of experience helping people and companies achieve their goals.

My accomplishments at the time included several years-worth of project and people management. I also had years of counseling multiple employees, peers, and clients under my belt. What's another word for counsel? Oh yeah, *coach*. And as my pal Shakespeare says, "A rose by any other name would smell as sweet." So, that settles that.

I can't charge for this? Um, yeah, I can — look how qualified I am!

And so, I made it (progress) until I made it (success). At first, I took on smaller projects to build my client list and gain further experience "as a coach". I took my business knowledge and personal experience and created actionable success plans (that worked!). I took every chance I had to network and secured a few speaking gigs at local events. Then I began to actively seek additional speaking opportunities. Eventually my reputation grew and I was asked to share my story and knowledge at larger events and at digital summits with attendees from around the world.

How to "Make It"

Everything I did was *deliberate*. Every decision I made was *calculated*. My every move was filled with *intention*. There was no room for faking it. This book is a testament to the things I've done and continue to do to make it, but there are a few honorable mentions that are worth a shout out, and may be worth a try, if you're wondering how to make it 'til you make it yourself.

Envision success. It's not enough to think positively, you've got to picture positive outcomes. One of my guiding principles is that I need *to see it to achieve it*. If I can picture it, I become committed to making it a reality. After I first interviewed for the marketing gig, it took almost a month for them to make their decision. In that time, I drove by the office almost every day and I told myself that I was going to work there. I would look up from the street below and imagine myself in the building looking down. I had dreams about making tea in the breakroom and spent time scouting out the parking options on all the side streets. In my mind, there was no *if*, there was only *when*. Those visuals encouraged me to saunter into my second interview as if the job was mine already, and they prompted me to write a follow-up email that eventually and *finally* landed me the position.

Positive thinking or the law of attraction alone isn't what will make you successful. You've got to take deliberate action. When you envision *it*, in some corner of your brain, *it* becomes real, and you'll be inspired to do whatever is necessary to bring *it* out of your head and into the world.

Dress for the job you want, not the job you have. This sounds cliché, but I'm telling you, it works. When I started out as a Marketing Coordinator, I was fresh out of school and my wardrobe made that obvious. At the time, I was relegated to a corner office shared by three other people on a floor that was undergoing renovations. I was pretty much forgotten by the rest of the company; I may as well have been in the supply closet. Six months into the job, people still didn't know who I was when I went downstairs to attend meetings. I felt as frumpy as the old torn-up carpet beneath my feet. This did not fly.

So, I decided it was time for a change, and I gave myself a makeover: I traded leggings for dresses, and flats for heels; I dyed my hair; I changed my diet and lost 20 pounds. By the time I was moved down to one of the renovated floors, I had undergone an entire transformation. I was walking taller, and it wasn't just the heels. I felt confident, and it cascaded into every area of my life. My newfound confidence is what paved the path for the five promotions that were waiting just around the corner for me.

Choose happiness. Yes, it's a choice. Making that choice is a form of cognitive therapy that encourages you to *think* positively in order to *feel* positively. You can choose to be miserable or you can choose to be happy, but you've got to make that choice, every day. You know those days when you wake up and think, *today is going to be GREAT!* and it turns out as such? That's the power of choice. Choosing to be happy requires you to consciously step away from the thoughts and triggers of a hopeless mindset and to step into environments that increase your probability for feeling happiness. Healthy relationships with family and friends, socializing, and regularly doing physical exercise make the choice easier. Focusing on the things that make us happy and allowing ourselves to be enthused by them helps us to shape a better perception of others and of ourselves, and contributes to our success.

Good vibes only. Choosing happiness requires a positive mindset. And in order to be positive, you've got to let the negative shit go. Inactiveness, indecision, and procrastination don't attract positivity. Thinking negatively is such a misuse of your imagination. Think of what you could accomplish if only you let goodness in. To do so, you may need to make some difficult changes; this may be your thoughts, it could be your belongings, and often times it's the people you're surrounded by.

Box above your weight. When I was young, I moved to a new province with my family. I was in a new school with a different curriculum and my grades started to slip, as did my self-assurance. My teacher saw that I was growing evermore defeated and taught me a lesson that I've carried with me well into adulthood: whether you think you can or you can't, you're right. If I kept telling myself that I wasn't going to get it, that I wasn't smart enough, or that it was too hard, I would fail the class and prove myself right. However, if I told myself that I'd catch up, that the material would begin to make more sense the more I'd study and that it would get easier over time, then I would motivate myself to keep going, and again, I'd prove myself right. Perhaps I was young and easily influenced, or perhaps my inner Boss was starting to blossom, but at that moment, I immediately switched to a *"yes I can"* mentality. As my confidence grew, I began to think beyond my perceived abilities and pushed myself even further. Since then, there has never been a mountain that I've deemed too high to climb.

I didn't climb the corporate ladder by aiming low. I went after a job that I wasn't yet qualified for. I didn't have all the necessary skills to run a department at the time, but I believed I could do it, and I genuinely felt that I was their best option. I was honest with my boss: I knew my strengths and weaknesses and walked into the interview as if the job was already mine. I didn't have a marketing degree or years of experience, but I had guts and was willing to put in the work to better myself. I'm grateful to have had a manager that helped me to grow into the position and prepare me for the challenges that lay ahead. She was a strong woman in a man's world, whose guidance continues to serve me. Much like a fighter who trains before stepping into the ring with someone larger, I practiced. With her help, and with the help of many others, I got stronger, I learned new techniques, and I've been ducking punches and raising the bar ever since.

Gamble. When it comes to making yourself big, you've got to believe you can do it. There will be times where you'll question whether you should hold 'em or fold 'em. Remember, you're betting on yourself. This is ultimately the best (and safest) bet you'll ever make. If you're not convinced, consider this: there's no amount of betting against yourself that will lead you to success. There's nothing that belittling your dreams or playing small can do to make you happier. Success is yours for the taking, but you've got to go all-in.

At the end of your life, do you want to reflect on how safely you played the game or on what it felt like to win? You might occasionally lose a hand, but when you bet on yourself, you'll still win the game.

Stay challenged. If you don't feel challenged, there's a good chance you're going to get bored, and boredom gets in the way of making it. Boredom often stems from repetitiveness, from not having a goal to work toward, or from a lack of passion for what you're doing. This is as true in relationships as it is in the workplace. Keep a healthy dose of challenge in your life by learning new skills, incorporating fulfilling tasks into your everyday routine, and embracing new things.

Starting my own business was the best thing I could do to keep myself challenged. I had no intention of "firing my boss"; I had nothing against the nine to five lifestyle; I didn't feel like I was settling for building someone else's dream—but I wanted to remain challenged and I wanted to wake up happy every day. So, I built a business that would allow me to do just that. It certainly has challenged me, in more ways than I anticipated, but it has been one of my greatest sources of happiness as well.

In case you need the reminder: success is not hiding in your comfort zone.

Get excited. Something I consciously do when I'm nervous, whether I'm about to step onstage or out of a plane, is to shift my nervousness to excitement. I know that, generally, if I'm nervous about something, it's because I *really* want it. And *really* *wanting* something can be scary. I recently watched a video of Mel Robbins, CNN contributor, author and my spirit animal, explaining the difference between fear and excitement. She spoke about the studies that have been done that prove that physiologically, being excited is exactly the same as being afraid. Our bodies simply don't know the difference. In both scenarios, our bodies react the same way with racing hearts, rising temperatures, or that feeling we get in the pit of our stomach right before the roller coaster drops. The only difference between the two scenarios is what your brain is telling you: if you don't train your brain to embrace excitement, it's going to tell you something is wrong instead, and you'll become ridden with fear. Her advice was to frame a context for your brain in those moments so that it doesn't jump into fearfulness. Hype yourself up and tell yourself that everything you're experiencing at that moment is happening because you want it to happen. Think of all the positive things that led you to that moment and what you stand to gain from it. This will boost your confidence and allow you to do more of what you set out to do.

Some people are born with confidence, others must learn it, but it *can* be taught. Being confident isn't simply feeling assured that things will work out; it's the willingness to try to make things work out. Define your goal, figure out what it's going to take to achieve it, and start making it a reality, little by little. That's the Bossing Up Life.

"Some people want it to happen, some wish it would happen, others make it happen." – Michael Jordan

Notes

Chapter 20
Your Tribe Affects Your Vibe

You Can't Do Epic Shit with Basic People

We're inherently tribal; we do better in packs, it's that simple. But somewhere in our evolution we began to value independence more than we did support. We work ourselves into a state of stress and isolation trying to do it all, and for what? They say it takes a village to raise a child; well, it takes a village to be successful, too. And the people you surround yourself with dramatically impact your vibe. Whether we like it or not, our way of thinking, our self-esteem, and our decisions are greatly influenced by our environments and the people who inhabit them. If you're feeling stuck or uninspired, take a look around you. They say we're the sum of the five people we spend the most time with and sometimes those people are just… uninspiring. But *their* reality doesn't have to be *your* reality. If you want to make significant changes in your life, then you must surround yourself with living examples who prove those changes are possible. Attend local meetups, join online communities, say yes to opportunities that will connect you with like-minded people; they *will* propel you forward.

What's great about your tribe is that they don't "need" to be by your side, they chose to be. They get your inability to settle for the status quo because they, too, hunger for more. They genuinely support your quest for success and don't merely tolerate it. Those who are in your life by choice and positively contribute to your journey are a special kind of people. They will give you the real talking to you need (though you may not always want it) to stay on track. They will be there to celebrate your wins and help you get through your losses. They know your strengths and your shortcomings and will help you keep your eye on the prize. They're there to call you on your bullshit, keep you accountable, and stop you from playing small or rationalizing away your dreams. Your vibe has equal impact on them as well; it's a two-way street. As such, you can't rely solely on them to lift you up; you need to put in the work daily to be your best self, not only for yourself, but for those who rely on your support. Your vibe is key to your success, and to theirs.

Bossing Up in Action

Petrona Joseph, TV personality and Author, New York, NY

"Growing up, my dad always said to my sisters and me: "birds of a feather flock together." I never quite understood what he meant at the time, but in hindsight I can pinpoint how the different situations in my life attracted the people that were in it at the specific time.

Your vibe is everything. The key to succeeding in life can be summarized in one idea: like attracts like. What are you attracting? Be honest with yourself and make a list of everything you've recently let gravitate towards you. Were they quality people? What about money? When was the last time you attracted a free flowing $2,000? Once you've completed your list, hold a meeting with yourself and recognize that everything that you have written down reflects who you are. You attract what you are. Once you have taken stock of your reflection, adjust what needs to be adjusted. Are your desires aligned with what you have been emitting to the Universe? To be abundant, think abundantly and give freely. You will attract abundance. To be happy and to attract happiness, think happy thoughts.

The power of thought is incredible, and it has helped me succeed. Every morning, no matter my mood, I throw the mantra "I am love" into the atmosphere—and so I am."

Not Everyone Is Tribe Material

Some people have different values, some are just sour about life, and others have an indignant "how dare you" attitude because they feel threatened by your determination or are jealous of it. Does this sound like your partner, your parent, or your boss? Even someone so close to you may be the one who's holding you back. If so, assess what you can do to improve the relationship to get it to a point where it's a source of positivity and encouragement in your life. If you feel you've done everything you can and yet they still drain the ambition from your veins, don't feel guilty for putting yourself first and seeking a tribe that mirrors your potential. You'll be a better parent, person or professional (or all of the above), when you're living true to yourself and surrounded by people who support your mission.

But don't panic: when quitting your job, ending your relationship, or repairing the rift with your parent isn't a viable option, rest assured that there are online communities for *everything*. Whether you're into remodeling cars, winter camping, or day trading, there's a community for that. Our tribes can span the world, thanks to the glorious World Wide Web, and online communities are revolutionizing the way people connect, who otherwise would have never met. They're a great way to learn different perspectives, cultures, and tips from people who are dealing with similar challenges to the ones you're facing.

No matter how self-sufficient you believe yourself to be, the truth remains that *even you* need a tribe. I love online communities and connecting with likeminded people over topics I'm interested in or passionate about. Some of the ones I'm part of that closely reflect my interests include:

- Local foodie groups; we share the best festivals and restaurants in my city
- Local networking groups; we share upcoming events and discuss key takeaways from past events
- Fitness groups; we do daily check-ins and discuss the progress and struggles of our fitness journey
- Blogging groups; we discuss ways to optimize and monetize our blogs, as well as help each other promote most recent posts
- Webinar groups; we share different webinars that are relevant for entrepreneurs as well as best practices on how to make money while we sleep
- Travel groups; we share photos, experiences and itineraries
- Bossing Up, duh!

To maximize the benefits of online communities and build a valuable virtual tribe, follow these five rules:

1. Always introduce yourself and then follow up with a question to learn something about the other members.
2. Genuinely engage with the other members of the community by liking and commenting on the posts that resonate with you.
3. Ask for advice and leverage the wisdom of the group.

4. Offer advice when you're asked and own that you're a valuable member of the community.

5. Always be respectful of the community's rules and of the feelings of its members.

Bonus: Take it offline when possible; nothing beats face-to-face interaction with people who get you.

It's so inspiring to get daily updates on what people are doing to better their lives, build their businesses, and explore new opportunities. The high I feel from a shared intuition and valued ideas has kept me going on days where I was just not feeling it. My tribe, both virtually and locally, has kicked my motivation into high gear and have made a world of difference in achieving my goals.

"If you want to travel fast, go alone. If you want to travel far, go together." - African proverb

Notes

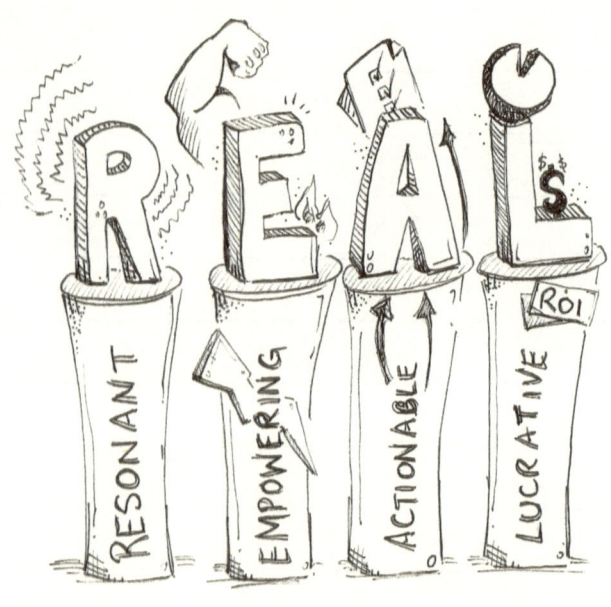

Chapter 21
REAL Talk

A New Way of Setting (and Keeping) Goals

Like a hamster on a wheel, so many of us work hard, but don't feel we get anywhere worthwhile. If that's an accurate description of your current mood, it's likely that you haven't clearly identified what you want and have therefore not set appropriate goals to get it. Goal-setting is a powerful process that helps to plan for a preferred outcome and sparks the motivation necessary to turn that vision into reality. Yet it's greatly underutilized and often poorly executed.

You need to commit to a plan to achieve your goals. This doesn't mean that your plan can't change. It means that setting your goals cannot start and end with a declaration; it requires action.

Following a plan provides you with a sense of accomplishment. With that feeling comes increased self-confidence, greater happiness, and more success. Anyone can do it, no matter what their objective is. But in order for you to experience all that goodness, you need to find a system that works for you; one that you *want* to follow.

Challenging the Status Quo:

Perhaps you're familiar with the SMART goal method as a means of setting and adhering to objectives. The acronym has taken many forms over the years, but most commonly stands for Specific, Measurable, Achievable, Realistic and Time-bound. The SMART approach is easy to understand and easy to measure; it's basically a glorified checklist. You map out what you want to do, how you're going to do it, and when you want it done. It's cognitive in nature, making it ideal for project management and performance management, but it falls short on emotion. Simply put, it lacks *passion*, and if you're not passionate about your goals, you won't feel successful.

How many times have you set SMART goals (or an equivalent) for yourself, worked on them for a week, and then left them to collect dust, along with your New Year's resolutions from '08?

Now think about how many times you set SMART goals in which you felt emotionally invested, I mean *really* invested, the kind of invested that catapults you out of bed every day before your alarm goes off, the kind that you feel flowing through your veins and fueling your every move. Not many, huh? That's because passion is the secret sauce to goal setting; without it life's going to taste pretty bland. Passion forces you to think about the "why." Not why you *want* to do something, but why it *matters* to you that you do it, and if it matters enough to you to continue doing it when life throws shit your way. When you know why it matters, you're much more likely to stay accountable. When you frame your goals within the context of your life plan, the direct impact they will have on your happiness and success becomes that much more evident. It's much harder to put your happiness and success on a shelf than it is a checklist.

I like SMART goals but I felt certain there was a better way to connect myself emotionally to my goals and stay more accountable to them, so I began to search for another method to serve as a constant reminder of my "why". I was looking for a framework that would help me envision my goals and compel me to take immediate action. I didn't want a to-do list; I wanted to *feel* something when I envisioned my goals. I flipped through books, read countless articles, and Googled things that returned questionable results (the Internet is a scary place), but I always came up empty-handed.

I knew there must be an answer; why couldn't I find it? Then I heard a click, and this time it wasn't my mouse. A light went off in the attic of my mind. I couldn't find the answer in a book or online because it was still living in my head—I had it. So, I listened inward and began to connect the dots. What I've developed, and have now been practicing for several years, is the REAL goal methodology.

Resonant

Empowering

Actionable

Lucrative

'REAL' is an acronym for emotionally-stimulating criteria that guide you to develop objectives that matter. Given that your goals and emotions change according to their context, this approach focuses more on accountability rather than trackability and supports more active engagement with your goals than simply measuring them would allow. The REAL goal framework has been the foundation of every single one of my adult accomplishments. It has consistently enabled me to remain accountable, achieve what I set out to do and has been the catalyst for ongoing success.

Time to Get REAL... here's how to use the methodology

1. **Resonant.** Setting goals is easy, sticking to them is harder. Develop goals that resonate with your core and vibe with your values. Tying your goals to your values serves as a constant reminder of why you're pursuing them. If you're struggling to connect your goals to your values, reconsider the impact that goal has on achieving your version of success.

2. **Empowering.** Your goals need to be more than just a to-do list. To feel truly empowered, develop goals that embody your strengths, and leverage them to help you make progress. Every time you think of your goal, you should be reminded of your ambition to do more, learn more, and *be* more.

3. **Actionable.** To achieve success, you must break down your goals into actionable steps. Many people quit before they begin to see progress because they're intimidated by a mountain of a goal. Breaking down your goals into smaller steps allows you to remain challenged enough to keep your interest without setting yourself up to fail. Having identified your strengths, you can start with steps you know you'll do well. Accomplishing those steps early on triggers positive behavioral momentum, and builds your confidence as the steps become more challenging.

4. **Lucrative.** When developing your goals, be a little selfish and think about what's in it for you and *why* that matters. You must profit from your goals, whether you learn something new, let go of old behaviors, or turn a profit on your idea. Establishing what you'll gain from achieving your goals makes it easier to work toward them. Ask yourself this question often to ensure that your goal is still serving you.

As an example, one of my goals is to grow my coaching practice. The REAL goal I've set for myself is as follows:

Resonant: Continue to build a coaching practice that offers significant value to people seeking help in achieving success in their personal and professional lives (being a person of value is one of my core values).

Empowering: Use my experience, my voice, and my platforms to share my knowledge, equip others to surpass their expectations of themselves, and constantly learn from their experiences.

Actionable: Work on and evolve this list weekly:

- Evaluate speaking opportunities.
- Source new speaking opportunities.
- Update calendar with new events.
- Create new content for my blog.
- Work on creating an online offer.
- Strategize video marketing plan.
- Attend webinars or seminars to continuously learn.

- Evaluate email marketing strategy.
- Build a distribution plan for *Bossing Up*.
- Plan a book tour.

Lucrative: Here are three examples of *what's in it for me* and *why they matter*:

What's in it for me: Benefitting from learning about different industries, products, and services, and expanding my value as a professional.

Why that matters: Continuously learning and staying current enables me to be selective and take on projects that excite me and that I want to learn more about. Having that liberty is one of the things I like most about having my own business.

What's in it for me: Generating an income by doing something that gives me a great sense of purpose and fulfillment.

Why that matters: It allows me to do what I love every day, it finances other projects I care deeply about, and it allows me to pursue the things I have always wanted to do.

What's in it for me: Having the opportunity to regularly meet new and fascinating people.

Why that matters: I really enjoy making genuine connections with people. Connections allow me to build my network and get people on board the Bossing Up movement. Connections also allow me to support the movements of others, resulting in a greater sense of connectedness to my community.

When I look at my REAL goal and at the importance it has on my everyday happiness, as well as the impact it can have on my immediate and long-term success, it becomes *tangible*. My passion seeps through into every word, and that's impossible for me to put off or ignore.

Taking REAL Action

Plan for "failure." Wait, what? Isn't this book about planning for success?

You *will* inevitably encounter some roadblocks or full-on road closures on your journey to success, so it helps to plan accordingly. If you haven't yet heard of prospective hindsight and the concept of the "pre-mortem", allow me to blow your mind. Prospective hindsight is the act of imagining that an event has already occurred. A pre-mortem requires you to imagine that your journey has gone horribly wrong before it has even begun, and to hypothesize about *why* that happened. Doing so allows you to identify risk of failure from the onset and to take proactive steps to reduce them.

The first step of the exercise is to choose a major project, decision, or life change to focus on. The next step is to list every realistic cause of derailment that you can foresee. In case you were wondering, an alien invasion does not classify as realistic. It's important to recognize both external as well as internal factors that can hinder your success. This will prime you to pick up on early signs of derailment once your plan is in motion.

For example, if you're planning on starting a business, you may want to take the following factors into consideration:

Extrinsic

- Economic downturn
- Lack of a proper business plan
- Insufficient savings
- Incomplete competitor research
- Limited knowledge of target audience

Intrinsic

- Self-defeating thoughts and tendencies
- Poor time management
- Fear of, or unwillingness, to ask for help
- Gets bored easily
- Laziness

Do note that internal factors are often completely overlooked when setting goals. Don't make this mistake. Let's face it, we're often our own biggest roadblock and we need to know when to get out of our own way.

Once your extrinsic and intrinsic factors are mapped out, you'll have a clear picture of the challenges you face, and, with some foresight, what will be required to overcome them. Prioritize the top ten challenges you foresee as the *most likely* to deter your ability to succeed and work their solutions into your plan.

While I still find value in the SMART methodology for tactical goals such as creating a marketing plan or working against (writing) deadlines, REAL goals have better served me for my intrinsic, big-picture goals. Contextualizing my goals within the pre-mortem exercise has allowed me to reach new heights. I feel more prepared, humbled, and confident in the execution of my goals. Give it a shot —what's the best that could happen?

"The trouble with not having a goal is that you can spend your life running up and down the field and never score." - Bill Copeland

Notes

Notes

Embracing ~ the ~ Bossing Up Life

Part 5: Embracing the Bossing Up Life

"Incredible change happens in your life when you decide to take control of what you do have power over instead of craving control over what you don't." — Steve Maraboli

As you must have discovered by now, Bossing Up is a way of life. It's a combination of flexing your assertiveness, making positive choices, and taking action that empowers you and those around you. If you're still reading this book, I think it's safe to assume that you have insatiable passion, a hunger for more, and an unrelenting curiosity about how to bring it all together.

No matter what journey you're on, the fact that this book is even before your eyes proves that you're already Bossing Up, and that you're ready to cultivate that curiosity and start the next chapter in your Bossing Up story.

These principles will help.

Notes

Chapter 22
Bro, Do You Even Lift?

Lift and Be Lifted. There's Room for Everyone to Win

A healthy dose of competitiveness sparks a certain fire in us that's sometimes needed to put thought into action. Checking the scoreboard can serve as good inspiration to push harder and continuously improve. However, when competitiveness and comparison collide, it creates a toxic mindset.

Our pursuit of power and success often tricks us into comparing ourselves to others, and, as a result, we become preoccupied with fear and envy. Using those emotions as motivation to succeed can actually interfere with success. Extrinsic motivation drives us to do things outside of our personal motives for the reward rather than for the passion we feel for our achievements; being rewarded on those behaviors reduces our intrinsic motivation because we get so caught up on "winning" that we forget what we're doing it for.

Comparison is the thief of joy... don't you want to keep your joy? There will always be competition, whether it's a colleague striving for the same promotion or another product that's claiming market share. There are healthy ways, however, to maintain your competitive advantage without becoming consumed with beating your opponent.

Be sensible. Praise and loyalty aren't finite resources. I repeat: praise and loyalty **are not** finite resources. We know this in theory, but it's time to let it really sink in. To understand that there's no shortage of opportunity in this world to succeed could make it easier for you to consider your competitors as the impetus for innovation rather than as your impending doom. Come to your senses, stop comparing, acknowledge your fears and your reasons for jealousy, and use them to reflect on how you can improve and become more confident in yourself or your company. Jealousy cannot survive when you're confident and in pursuit of your own vision of success.

Embrace collaboration. While this may seem counterproductive at first, forging relationships with your competitors can actually enable you to achieve greater levels of success. Working *with* them can allow you to strengthen your skills and complement your own abilities in the eyes of your employer or client. Your collective performance reflects well on you both, as it proves that you have their best interest in mind rather than your own. This establishes trust, loyalty, and may lead to additional opportunities. When you're embarking on a collaboration, however, it's important to approach the endeavor in a non-threatening manner. Make sure it's mutually beneficial and built on mutual trust. If at any point you start to sense that either of your successes must come at the expense of the other, the collaboration will inevitably go bust. It's then best to immediately confront your collaborators or to part ways before any damage can occur.

Form co-opetitions. Working with your competition isn't always possible, or of interest, but they needn't become your enemy. A coopetition is the happy place between cooperative and competitive behaviors. Basic principles of co-opetition stem from game theory, which stipulates that when opponents play, though they are competing, they must respect the rules. In other words, opponents must cooperate with each other.

Dissimilar to traditional collaborations which require you to join forces to win together, coopetition encourages you to pool together your knowledge, skills, and resources, as well as to leverage the strengths of your competitor. Doing so can provide greater value to both parties and ensure that you both win.

A great example of co-opetition is that of LinkedIn's partnership with competing head hunters. Recruiters have grown accustomed to using LinkedIn to find prospective candidates and employment opportunities, and LinkedIn relies on recruiters to use and grow its platform. While they each would prefer to be solely responsible for placing their candidates, they recognize that the network of qualified applicants is larger when they both have skin in the game.

Another stellar example of co-opetition done right is Amazon's Marketplace. Amazon welcomes any and all competitors to use its e-commerce platform to sell their new and used products, alongside the same or similar products sold by Amazon itself. Using cooperative and competitive behaviors, the world's leading e-commerce site successfully leverages the strengths and offerings of its competitors. The marketplace continues to grow year after year and has become a major source of revenue for the company.

The Importance of Lifting Each Other Up

Lifting someone up is like being a spotter at the gym. A good spotter supports someone, yet still allows them to push themselves harder than they could safely do alone. A great spotter intervenes to assist with the lift and helps them to push even harder.

You can't get to the top alone. You'll need the help of others, and to obtain help, you must lift them in return. Not only will it make you feel good, it increases your chances for success in the following ways:

- Helping others builds your circle of trust and influence.
- Lifting others often results in an exchange of knowledge that can have an immediate impact in your work and life.
- It motivates others to lift you in return.
- Seeing how others push themselves encourages you to push yourself.
- Understanding their struggles helps keep you humble.

There's room for everyone to win, but you've got to properly strategize to stay in the game. Remain cognizant that their success isn't your loss, and that their loss will not necessarily guarantee your success. Choosing to support others rather than to spite them will always keep you in the game, even if it momentarily takes you out of the lead. But working with your competitors, in one form or another, often gets you ahead.

"Competition has been shown to be useful up to a certain point and no further, but cooperation, which is the thing we must strive for today, begins where competition leaves off."
— *Franklin D. Roosevelt*

Notes

Chapter 23
Trust Me, You Can Afford It

Investing in Yourself Always Yields ROI

To invest is to expend time or money with the expectation of achieving a higher return or profit. People want to get the most of their minutes and dollars, and those who invest wisely have their time and money working for them. It's no wonder the investment industry is worth hundreds of millions of dollars a year. There are experts around the globe who exist solely to guide your investment decisions, diversify your portfolio, and promise to earn you a decent return over time. While they may hold up their end of the bargain, they've neglected to tell you about the *best* investment you can make—investing in yourself.

We work in order to keep the companies we work for functional and agile (even if we work for ourselves), and in return we're paid for our time. Time is money, after all. That's an interesting statement, isn't it? Have you ever thought about what it really means? Time is a commodity, a truly valuable resource. If you think of time as money, then it would be well advised to spend it on the things that give us the results we desire and that create better results over time, as compound interest does. Ask yourself how you're spending your time and what you're doing to invest it in the only sure thing there is: *you*.

You can't advance on your personal or professional success journey without making some form of investment. You can't expect bigger and better with the same knowledge, the same way of thinking, and the same behaviors; you'll end up getting the same results. Surprise, surprise! Investing in yourself is making the conscious choice to spend time or money to positively affect your mind, body, and soul so you can grow. This goes well beyond purchasing those new sunglasses you've been eyeing (though by all means you should get them, they make you look fabulous). It's about making a commitment to be better today than you were yesterday, and that often requires learning new skills and behaviors that will drive you to the results you're looking for and then some. The best part is that you don't have to write a check to yourself in order to invest in your future.

Investing in yourself sends a powerful message to yourself and to those around you:

> *I'm worthy of all that I desire, I'm capable of achieving it all and I'm going to give it the energy, time, and effort needed to become a reality.*

Whoa, that's a pretty loaded statement—as it should be. If you're left thinking, *Yeah, that sounds great, but I don't know where to begin*, don't worry, I've got your back. These are my ten favorite ways to invest in myself:

1. **Get out and network.** Seminars and conferences are great because they allow you to attend crash courses on various industries, professions, and projects. They offer you the opportunity to learn a great deal and meet new people who share similar interests and a drive for self-development. Networking events can be costly, so if you're not in a position to dish out your dollars regularly in order to mingle, start a small-scale meetup within your network and encourage attendees to bring a guest. Investing your time

and money into expanding your network can pay off big for your personal and professional goals.

2. **Join an online community.** Online communities have completely transformed the networking scene and are particularly great for introverts who want to meet more people, but don't much care for crowds and cocktails. It doesn't matter if you're in the heart of New York City surrounded by people or deep in Alaska with polar bears for neighbors. As long as you have WIFI, you too can join a group and benefit from its collective knowledge and expertise.

3. **Join a club.** Local club gatherings are more intimate than networking events and online communities, and can therefore offer you more genuine connections. Get together with others to discuss business, review books you've read, or go running around the neighborhood. Identify an activity that makes you happy and join the club, or choose something new you'd like to try and do more of it. If such a club doesn't already exist, start one. Being around positive, like-minded people will motivate you to invest in yourself more regularly.

4. **Go to the library.** I just recently went to my local library and discovered, much to my surprise, that libraries are making a comeback and are actually kind of …cool! Did you know that you can rent books and read them on your phone or tablet? Some libraries are even adopting the co-working movement; they may also offer workshops, coffee and baked goods. The library has come a long way from the place in high school where all the seniors made their fake

IDs (guilty, sorry mom). Check out a library near you to see how it's evolved. Rent a book, have a latte, and learn something new.

5. **Listen to podcasts.** One of the biggest reasons why people claim they're unable to do more for themselves is that they "don't have time." Well, you have two choices: you've got to *make* the time, or make the *most* of the time you've got. This is where mastering the micro moments comes in handy. Whether you're commuting to work, on a flight, or pumping iron, trade your Dance Mix '96 playlist for a podcast that can keep you-up-to-date with the latest news in your industry, broaden your perspective, or inspire you to take action.

6. **Take advantage of online materials.** One of my favorite ways to invest in myself is through online materials. I try to listen to two webinars a week on varying topics, some for personal interests, others for professional growth. I take advantage of every relevant eBook, checklist, or free training course that comes my way (and I sometimes get suckered into paying for the good ones!). I watch tutorials, I sign up for classes, I'm obsessed with TED Talks—I absorb as much information as possible and use it to validate existing ideas, spark new ones, gain a new perspective, remain relevant, and learn how others are achieving success.

7. **Make health a priority.** Exercise, proper eating, and sleep are the first routines to be pushed down the totem pole of life when I get busy. I've learned that this is a dangerous trifecta. Letting just one of those things slip directly impacts

everything else I do, and letting them all go at once is disastrous. Making (and keeping) them a priority is the best way to ensure that I'm getting the most from my other investments. I make small efforts every day to keep my health in check, like having a healthy breakfast every morning, exercising regularly, packing my lunch and snacks as much as possible when I'm on the road, and spending as much time outdoors, getting some extra walking in, as possible. This allows me to remain focused, stay energized, and ultimately be more productive.

8. **Carve out some alone time.** This might seem like a fluffy investment, but a little alone time can go a long way. Get a massage, go for a relaxing drive, read, write. Whatever you do, make time for yourself. You need it to recharge and reconnect with your thoughts and emotions to make sure you're still on track. Every other investment you make will not yield as high a return if you're no longer on the best path for you.

9. **Indulge a little.** It's good to indulge once in a while. Brag a little, have the brownie, take a nap, turn on Netflix, buy the shoes. If you're working hard, you should reward yourself. Don't feel guilty for celebrating: just make sure to celebrate within reason. I like to think about how I'm going to treat myself ahead of time so that I have a little something extra to look forward to. Investing in those extra incentives helps to keep my morale high and gives me a little something to show or experience as a result of all my hard work. A little positive reinforcement never hurt anyone.

10. **Work with a coach.** A good coach is an invaluable resource for your personal and professional growth. Working with a coach is a worthwhile investment, as they:

- Act as a sounding board.

- Help you to discover new things about yourself.

- Focus on positive behavioral change.

- Facilitate personal and professional development.

- Build valuable skills and knowledge that you can use to achieve your goals.

- Offer you support and encouragement when you're faced with new challenges.

- Address derailing behavior and help you to tackle difficult issues in a safe environment

- Empower you to cut through the clutter, find your best self, and propel it forward.

- Provide you with the inspiration and guidance you need to stay accountable to your commitment to yourself.

- Help you to identify your weaknesses and factor them into your success plan.

- Enhance problem analysis.

- Train you to mitigate feelings of low self-worth and frustration.

- Encourage personal learning, responsibility, and insight.

Investing in yourself will provide you with the skills, knowledge, and motivation necessary to combat negative thoughts and behaviors and to encourage positive ones. Like any good portfolio, the best investments you make in yourself must be diversified, managed carefully and frequently, and reap long term benefits. Keep your REAL goals in mind and invest accordingly.

"Invest in as much of yourself as you can, you are your own biggest asset by far." – Warren Buffet

Notes

Notes

Chapter 24
A Balanced Life Is Overrated

Finding the Beauty in Imbalance

A balanced life is an elusive concept to most. Many of us feel that we should work less, spend more time with family, or make time for more fun. We hear a lot about the importance of a work-life balance, as if there was a clear divide between the two, but not as much about what other areas of our lives may need some fine-tuning and how to achieve that.

How is it that balance, something we think is so critical to our happiness and success, has become a universal struggle and seems to cause us more guilt and stress than peace of mind? I would argue that it's because we aren't looking at the big picture and are neglecting key components.

It takes more than a weekend away or going on a technology detox to reignite our flame when it's burning low. While those things certainly help to replenish us, their benefits are short-lived. You need to check in with yourself regularly to assess which areas of your life are out of whack. Without insight into the areas that are falling short, your stress level will rise and you'll inevitably burn out, no matter how invincible you think you are. When I feel my happiness, productivity, or energy slipping, I evaluate eight key areas of my life that I consider to be my pillars of success.

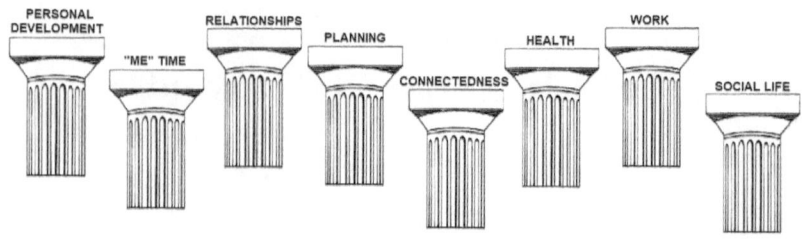

Assessing Balance (or Lack Thereof) with the Success Pillar Quiz:

If something is off and you can't quite pinpoint it, you may be underestimating how many contributing factors there are to your happiness and success, and you may be neglecting small things that can have a significant impact. Knowing how your pillars align is half the battle, so let's have a little fun and see how they're helping or hindering your ability to succeed.

Rate yourself from one (you need to up your game) to ten (your game is tight) in the following areas. Then check the boxes of the areas in which you're doing well (rated six or higher) and leave the boxes blank in the areas you need to improve (rated five or lower).

Personal Development

- Emotional intelligence
- Ongoing education
- Reading
- Motivation
- Self-esteem
- Fulfillment

"Me" Time

- Arts & music
- Literature
- Rest & leisure
- Sports & hobbies
- Travel & vacation
- Humor & fun

Relationships

- Parents
- Children
- Relatives
- Spouse
- Intimacy/sex
- Parenting

Planning

- Financial planning
- Time management
- Goal setting
- Life transitions
- Career planning

Aging & Mortality

- Connectedness
- Morals and ethics
- Living an authentic life
- Connection to nature or a higher power
- Forgiveness
- Gratitude
- Meditation

Health

- Physical fitness
- Nutrition
- Stress reduction
- Medicine & healing
- Sleep
- Healthy living

Work

- Happiness at work
- Workplace relationships
- Business skills
- Entrepreneurship/intrapreneurship

- Management skills
- Leadership

Social Life

- Friends
- Trying new activities
- Community involvement
- Communication skills
- Listening skills
- Sharing & generosity
- The environment

Once you know which areas of your life require some improvement, it's time to take the necessary steps to *actually* improve them. Devoting energy to *all* these areas and unleashing your true potential is possible with these tools:

Take accountability. Ask yourself why certain areas of your life rank lower than you'd like them to; be honest. Is your home life suffering because you're working too much? Have you abandoned a personal project because you lack the motivation to complete it? Do you want to give back to the community, but you just feel so lazy? Understand what's getting in your way and think about what changes you can make to regain control in those areas.

Set REAL goals. Control, or lack thereof, can sometimes be impalpable. Setting REAL goals can help make it feel more within reach. When you've lost control over certain areas of your life and are honest about how it's affecting you, you can set goals that are resonant, empowering, actionable, and lucrative to keep you in a Zen-like state.

Start making moves. You can't just think about how things ought to change, you've got to make some (potentially hard) choices and get the gears turning. Make it your mission to run the day rather than letting the day run you. Set your intentions and commit to them. Whether asking for help at work, attending workshops to reignite your passion, or asking someone to volunteer with you to keep you accountable, you need to take action. To avoid feeling overwhelmed, focus on one area at a time and introduce change in bite-sized chunks.

Set yourself up for success. If you're like me, you might be guilty of caving and paying mind to unnecessary intrusions. Do you have forty-eight tabs open on your computer, screaming for your attention when you've got *one thing* that needs your sole focus? Have you taken a day off to catch up on filing your taxes, but decide instead, *Well, I'm off, I might as well get what I need from the pharmacy… and IKEA?* Is your phone kept in sight, even when you're up against a deadline? Do yourself a favor and get rid of these distractions if you want to set yourself up for success. Part of achieving success is prioritizing your time and truly making your tasks a priority.

Speak up. You just don't know what you don't know. You can try to troubleshoot, problem solve, and justify things only according to the information that's in your ol' brain box. The best answers, however, aren't always there. That's why it's important to communicate regularly with those you trust. Listening to their perspective and gaining their insight can be especially helpful in assuring you're on the right path, or in making the choice to change direction, if needed.

Rinse and repeat. Doing this exercise once isn't a fix-all solution; it needs to become a routine check-in, just like every other health check. Life's circumstances will change, your motivation and priorities will fluctuate—that's normal. It's important to keep track of those changes in real-time to assess how they're impacting you and if they're causing you to get in your own way. Make it part of your weekly routine to see where you're slipping, and readjust.

The Beauty of Imbalance

All our lives, we're told that balance is a good thing. Our parents, peers and HR departments tell us we should strive to equalize all areas of our lives. But if you've ever taken a physics class, you've learned that balance is the neutralization of forces that end up in "status quo." In this state, there's either no movement or development, or if there is movement, it's being compensated by an opposite force.

In order to move or develop, we must create a certain type of imbalance. And us Bosses need to constantly move and develop. We've been so consumed by the balancing act when really, we ought to think about tipping the scale. Not everything needs, or even should, be balanced—hence the varying heights of my pillars. There's sufficient balance there to keep me elevated, but enough imbalance to accommodate some movement, and therefore growth.

I encourage you to revisit the results of your quiz and look at it through a different lens. Embrace the imbalance in your life and deliberately and carefully initialize movement in the areas in which you'd like to focus on more.

> *"There's no such thing as work-life balance. There are work-life choices, and you make them, and they have consequences."*
> *— Jack Welch*

Notes

Chapter 25
#Winning

How to Create Your Own Opportunities

We all have that friend or colleague who chalks up their success to being in the right place at the right time. This friend is always doing cool things and has stories that sound like they belong on the silver screen. It's always that same friend who keeps getting lucky, isn't it? The truth is, they didn't get lucky. It wasn't fate. Whether they realize it or not, they set themselves up for success and they're able to regularly achieve success because they know how to create and embrace it. The good news is, you don't need to be a rocket scientist to figure it out. Change just a few habits and *you* can be that friend, too.

Success is the Intersection of Preparation and Opportunity.

It's not enough to be in the right place at the right time. There will always be opportunities; you must be willing and able to see them, however, and be prepared to take action and let success in once it presents itself. Twitter co-founder Biz Stone, says, "I believe that you have to be the architect of the circumstances—that opportunity is something you manufacture, not something you wait for." So, how does one "architect the circumstances" and create opportunities for success? These ten powerful Bossing Up habits, which apply to entrepreneurs and intrapreneurs alike, will help you make your own luck every day of the week:

1. **Take pride in what you do.** Honoring your work and exuding confidence when you tell someone what you do will greatly shape their perception of you and your capabilities. Projecting pride leaves a strong and memorable impression that encourages people to look for opportunities where they could use your expertise.

2. **Practice humility.** As important as it is to take pride in what you do, you must remain humble. Opportunities present themselves more often when you're perceived as someone who cares equally about the impact you have on others as on your own personal gain. Don't get carried away with being who you think they want you to be. Being genuine will ensure that you create opportunities that resonate with who you are.

3. **Educate yourself.** Whether this is going back to school, taking an online course, regularly listening to webinars, or catching up on industry-relevant blogs, keep yourself in the know. The world is changing at a rapid pace and you need to constantly evolve to maintain your competitive advantage and know where and how opportunities can be created.

4. **Actively seek opportunities.** As mentioned earlier, there's no shortage of opportunity, but you've got to seek those that are the best fit for you. To do so, be aware of your surroundings and your impact on them. Put yourself out there, be conscious of how you conduct yourself, pay attention in meetings and conversations, and make note of how you can contribute in a meaningful way. Then take initiative.

5. **Contribute.** More opportunities become available when you put yourself out there and stand out from the crowd. Let your work speak for itself by setting up a blog, offering courses, speaking publicly, being active on community forums, or writing a book (ahem!). The more you offer your knowledge, the more you're trusted as a thought leader in your profession, and opportunity loves leaders.

6. **Maintain an attitude of gratitude.** Gratitude and optimism breed opportunity. This too is not luck or fate. Studies prove that more than 80 percent of people who are grateful and happy actually work harder, and therefore experience a higher rate of opportunity.

7. **Don't ignore your gut instinct.** Some opportunities will be no-brainers, others will require you to pause and assess what's on the table. Listen to your intuition in these moments and make a decision accordingly. Sleep on it, write a pros and cons list, or talk through your concerns; but do give your inner voice a chance to be heard.

8. **Be decisive.** When you're faced with an opportunity that unquestionably aligns with your REAL goals, jump on it. Rely on the skills that got you there, and push the limits of your comfort zone. A single great opportunity often leads to several others.

9. **Develop your plan.** Creating opportunity is just the beginning; the magic is in the execution. This is your time to shine. Combine the insight and passion that created the opportunity into something truly valuable. Embrace your imagination and put it to work to better the lives of those with whom you'll be engaging.

10. **Under-promise and over-deliver.** Following through on your commitments and going beyond them is an effective way of managing expectations and securing future opportunities.

Adopt these habits and you'll be the cool friend at the party with the you-won't-believe-what-just-happened story. But even better than that, you'll be winning around the clock.

Bossing Up in Action

Andrea Hausmann, Coco Haus, Los Angeles, CA

"Growing up, we're taught that if you work hard, good things will come. What was never specified was how hard and for how long you have to work. Most people reach a wall where the current struggle is not worth the end result. I love getting to that wall, taking my sledgehammer out and breaking it down, brick by brick. It was that thinking that made it possible for me to earn a work visa to move to the U.S. No one offered me a job, a plan or a promise that it would happen. What I did have was a burning desire to change my life for the better.

In order to get the money that I needed and have the flexibility in schedule to get my paperwork done, I had to move into my parents' house in the country and work for them full time at their home office. I had to give up all the things that I loved doing; there was no more shopping, socializing, eating at restaurants, beauty routine, or fun. I worked from 8am to 9pm, seven days a week for nine months straight. I sold everything I wasn't attached to or couldn't ship. I essentially gave up everything that I had built in 10 years of being a working photographer in Montreal in the hopes that, just maybe, I might find a better life somewhere else. Some thought I was crazy, others that I was completely unrealistic, and only a few were as excited about my journey as I was.

I'm an independent person and moving into a space with zero privacy is the last thing I would choose for myself. But I knew it was my choice to be there and that it was only temporary. I kept my goal in my mind and in my heart and trusted that I had what it took to get it done. Anytime someone would question what I was doing, I would talk about "Risking it for the Biscuit." People thought I was insane when I talked about my cookie. Then I asked them what their end goal was, what their biscuit tasted like, and all of a sudden everyone got it.

The other theory that really helped me through this tough time was this: anything can be accomplished with enough time and/or money. I knew that if I saved every penny and put every good hour to work, that I could reach my goal. I had an ideal date in my head when I wanted to move to the US, which of course came and went, but I still held this belief that it would happen. I dug deep within, harnessing my patience and pushed forward, knocking each brick down until finally I had a clear path. I did not want my story to be that of "so close," I wanted it to be "look what she did." If I had given up because it took too long, I never would have known how close I was to succeeding.

I now live in LA, rebuilding my career from scratch while developing new relationships in new social circles. The only map I have is the one I've written myself. Who knows how long it will take for me to build the life I've dreamed of, but what I do know is this: I can risk it for the biscuit, no matter how long it takes and how much it costs."

"It had long since come to my attention that people of accomplishment rarely sat back and let things happen to them. They went out and happened to things." - Leonardo Da Vinci

Notes

Chapter 26
Prepare to Get Schooled

Personal Branding 101

You might be thinking, *I'm not in marketing—this section doesn't apply to me.* WAIT! Before you skip ahead, I need to tell you something... you're wrong.

Marketing is no longer reserved exclusively for business activities; it's at the core of our interactions. Whether you're looking for a new job or a hot new date, you need to know how to market yourself. Whether you're going for the promotion or going to a networking event, you need to know how to market yourself. Whether you want to partner with someone on a project or you want to find an investor, you need to... well, you get the point.

When compatibility is viewed in its crudest form, we're our own brand attempting to market ourselves. In his *Fast Company* article, "The Brand Called You," Tom Peters explains, "Regardless of the business we happen to be in, all of us need to understand the importance of branding. We are CEOs of our own companies: Me Inc." Marketing ourselves can sometimes be perceived as ugly and greedy, and there are definitely ways to do marketing wrong. The goal, however, is to determine value and communicate it with society at large. When done properly, it's entirely effective. So, you see, everyone needs these skills today. Even some of the marketers reading this can learn a thing or two from the knowledge I'm about to drop.

Before we dive in, it's important to mention that marketing yourself may feel uncomfortable at first. It might require a change in attitude, or time to get used to it. In those moments, the following are some things to keep in mind:

- People hate to be sold, but they love to buy: marketing helps you to articulate your value rather than shoving it down people's throat.

- You're not going to find the opportunity of your dreams by hiding in your basement; you've got to put yourself out there to be discovered.

- Marketing your strengths exudes confidence, not greed.

- Remember, you're not a used car salesman selling a lemon to an unsuspecting family; you're communicating your worth.

- And you *are* worthy.

Alright, now it's time for the good stuff. Here's an introduction to personal branding that will help you to successfully market yourself in any situation. Class is in session.

Get comfortable with persuasion. Persuasion is not about deceiving someone or selling them on an idea, it's about confidently knowing what you have to offer and developing a shared sense of purpose and. To be a good persuader, you need to establish an emotional connection early in the relationship. Understanding the needs and goals of the person you're talking to will help strengthen that connection. It's important to be honest about your intentions and offer as much information as possible to help them make an informed, albeit guided, decision.

Shut up and listen. Yes, this is about you and *your* story, but if you go into a conversation with a script, ready for the kill, you risk missing critical cues that will help you to market yourself according to your audience. Asking open-ended questions makes the person you're speaking with feel important, it establishes trust, and it can potentially give you insight into what motivates them, what impresses them and where they're stuck. Weaving this information into the value you offer is an incredibly powerful technique.

Think of your brand as your reputation. Having a good reputation is key to your success, especially when you're entering new territories. Amazon's Jeff Bezos famously defines a brand as "what people say about you when you are not in the room." Building my brand and my reputation as a coach who is knowledgeable, trustworthy, and eager to help others achieve success, has enabled me to tap into my personal network for opportunities that I wouldn't have gotten as easily on my own. I've leveraged my reputation to get my foot in the door in order to speak with the right people, and it has carried the weight of my interactions. Your reputation is what you're judged on, and the truth is, we're all being judged. So, establish what you want to be known for, and think of every interaction that you have as an opportunity to strengthen your reputation.

Conduct a brand audit. Make a list of where you communicate your brand. Your list can include things like work, client consultations, charity events, your website, dating sites, social media, etc. Look at yourself through the lens of those you're engaging with, both online and in person. Do you stand out? Are there gaps or inconsistencies between what you portray and what you want to be? Can anything you're doing be misconstrued or perceived negatively? Identify what needs fixing and fix it.

Establish your USP. A USP stands for Unique Selling Proposition, or Unique Selling Point. A USP is essentially your brand promise, and articulating it regularly is an extremely effective way to stand out from the crowd. The goal here isn't necessarily to be the best, but to be different. You might think there's nothing particularly unique about you or that it's impossible to be truly unique in this day and age, but there's a popular meme going around now that addresses this perfectly, and it states: no one is you and *that* is your superpower. The great thing about a USP is that it doesn't need to be universally unique; it just needs to be unique to your audience. There's a lot of information out there about how to create a USP, but it all boils down to the following three steps:

1. Identify something you're passionate about.
2. Take inventory of your skillset and extract the skills that align with that passion.
3. Identify how you can use your skills to attract and help your audience.

Your USP is critical to your brand and should be something you unabashedly claim and exhibit in your daily life.

Craft an elevator pitch. Imagine you run into a former colleague on the subway and they ask what your new company does. You rapidly try to wrap your mind around what you do, recent developments currently underway, and the direction things are going in. By the time you begin to speak, your colleague has likely reached their stop and gets off. Opportunity lost! Sayonara, see ya later.

It helps to have practiced a short and memorable summary for situations like these. An elevator pitch enables you to explain something within the time a short elevator ride would take. Perhaps you've been in a job interview, on a date, or seeking buy-in for a project you need help getting off the ground, and you've been asked "So, tell me about yourself." A thirty to sixty second summary to set the tone for that conversation is all you need to initially convey the value you bring, confidently deliver your message, and encourage your listener to take action, whether it's securing the job, the next date or the interest to take the conversation further—or anything else in between.

These are the five key components of an effective elevator pitch:

1. **Engage your listener.** It doesn't matter if you work for a company or run one; when you're explaining who you are or what you do, show enthusiasm. After all, if you're not enthused about what you're sharing, why should they be? Another good way to engage your listener early is to open the pitch with a hook or a question (or both). This gets their attention and helps to make your pitch contextually relevant to them.

2. **Choose your language carefully.** You can't assume that everyone speaks your language, whether that's sales lingo or pilot-talk. Your pitch should be given in a way that anyone can understand and that piques interest. So, ditch the industry jargon and the buzzwords while you're at it. You don't want your listener to feel dumb or bored. Don't be

shy to take pride in your accomplishments; just be mindful to avoid articulating them in a boastful manner. It's okay to sound a little sales-y; you do want them to buy into you after all, but you don't want your listener to feel like they're watching a ShamWow infomercial.

3. **Be prepared.** Sometimes we can anticipate when we're going to be asked to explain who we are or what we do; other times we're caught off guard. For this reason, it's a good idea to practice your pitch, since you never know what opportunities are around the corner. Practicing your pitch encourages you to put a fresh spin on it, gain confidence in your delivery, and plan your spiel according to *various* preconceived scenarios. The goal here is to feel reassured, not rehearsed. Solicit feedback from your peers and adjust your pitch accordingly.

4. **Be memorable.** This is when your USP should shine. Explain what's different about you, or what you do differently from everyone else with the same title or type of company. You don't have to overthink this step or reinvent the wheel. Memorable elevator pitches are ones that are energetic, crisp, and personable. Remember, being *you* is your superpower; show them how you're going to save the world (or at least solve a problem)!

5. **Wrap it up.** Ultimately, you want to make sure that your pitch flows, captures the most important information you wish to share, and ends with an action item that will encourage your audience to become an active member of your network.

Here's an example of my elevator pitch using these tools.

Have you ever been so passionate and motivated to start something new, but not knowing where to start prevented you from starting at all?

Well, I work with people just like you, and combine coaching with almost a decade of marketing experience to build actionable success plans that help turn those ideas into action. I typically work with people who are striving for more success in their personal and professional lives, who just need a little help getting started and staying accountable to their goals.

My approach is based on my Bossing Up philosophy, which is essentially my blueprint for success that earned me five promotions in five years, allowed me to double my salary in the process, and empowered me to start my business. I have packaged it in a way that anyone can follow to achieve success, whatever that means to them. I love it because I get to help people build lives and businesses they're proud of, while simultaneously accomplishing that for myself.

You mentioned you were starting a side project. I'd love to go for coffee and see how I might be able to help get it off the ground.

Chances are they'll want to work with me, even if there's no immediate project in the pipeline. I might also be referred to someone else they know who could benefit from my services. And if nothing else, we exchange information and remain valued members of each other's networks.

Disclaimer: The five key components of an effective pitch mentioned above will help you summarize all your awesomeness in sixty seconds or less and captivate your listeners, leaving them with a lasting impression. However, for those with a company who are looking to craft a pitch to serve as more of an executive summary of their business to attract potential partners, investors, or members of the board, your pitch will need to take shape a little differently. It should include the following:

- A problem that's worth solving
- Your solution to that problem
- Your target market and their spending behavior
- Your competitors and your key differentiators (your USP)
- An overview of your team
- A financial summary and forecast
- Alternative measurements of success
- Passion and personality

Build a network. You've got to put yourself out there. It might seem scary, but being incredible won't help you if you're anonymous; you need a network. Your network is an important piece of your brand puzzle. As such, you must be purposeful about who you let into your circle. Your network should be a good representation of your best self and who you want to be. The people you let in become a solid foundation of support, brand advocates, and "door openers" to new possibilities. A strong network will help you to build and refine your brand by vetting ideas, sharing information, and offering critical insights and assistance that will better prepare you for what's ahead.

Strengthen your digital footprint. One of, if not *the* most powerful tool at your disposal to strengthen your brand is your digital presence. With it, you have the ability to leave your mark and make a real impact. Give your brand purpose by communicating it through every platform you engage with. Enhance your online presence by creating relevant content. Share your knowledge and expertise through bylined articles or blog posts of your own. Express yourself and your opinions via video and enable people to connect with you through different channels.

Provide value. In the world of economics and business, the "network effect" refers to the effect that one user of a good or service has on the value of that good or service to other people. A term popularized by the adoption of the telephone, the value of phones was driven by the number of people using them. Today, social media has taken the throne. Platforms like Twitter and Facebook are becoming increasingly valuable as more users join. If you're wondering where I'm going with this, here it is: you've got to provide value to your network to extract value from your network. Your network will only be as valuable as what you put into it.

Keep learning. One of the most powerful marketing tools (and life tools) is knowledge. Immerse yourself in what interests you to keep your passion alive and your marketability high. Intelligence isn't only sexy, it's the currency of our times. The more you know, the more valuable you are and the more valuable you are, the more opportunities become available. Stay up-to-date so you can stay top-of-mind.

Manage your brand. What are some of the brands you know and love? They have won your loyalty because they consciously manage their reputation. And just like them, you too need to manage what you're putting out in the world as a reflection of "you." The truth is, in branding yourself, perception is reality.

While growing in reputation and earning kudos are great perks of managing your business, the real benefit comes from getting ahead of your own brand to manage the public's perception of you.

I manage others' perceptions of my brand by following these best practices:

- Pay attention to how you affect those around you: look for verbal and nonverbal cues, or straight up ask for some honest feedback. Do more of what's positive and less of what's negative.

- Roll with the respected. This is yet another reason why your tribe is so important. Surround yourself with those who already have the reputation you aspire to have.

- Make yourself visible. Find opportunities to talk about or show the value you provide. Sit next to those from whom you want to learn or whose attention you seek, and always contribute to the conversation.

- Own up to your mistakes. Everyone makes them, it's okay. What's not okay is ignoring them or passing them off onto someone else. Apologize and work your ass off to build a standing that better reflects your enormous capabilities.

- Give it your all. Doing things to the best of your ability shows that you're committed, and if for whatever reason things don't work out, you'll know for your own peace of mind that you had done your absolute best.

- Don't force things. You're not going to knock it out of the park with everyone you meet. If they're someone you want in your circle, be genuine, be humble, and be patient.

Your reputation, and ultimately your brand, help you to show and articulate your value. In every situation, a strong reputation will help you to cut through the clutter and rise to the top.

"No matter what you do, your job is to tell your story."
- Gary Vaynerchuk

Notes

Notes

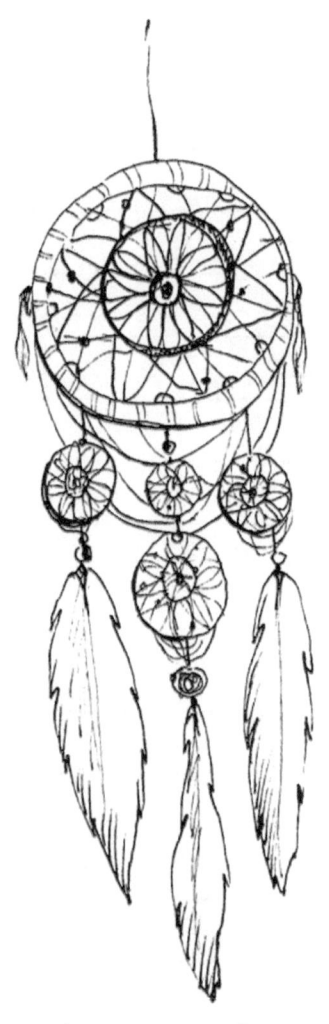

Chapter 27
You Might Suck

But You Might Be Great

There will come a time, or several times if I'm being honest, where nothing will seem to be going your way, and you'll contemplate throwing in the towel on the whole "success" thing. Even the hungriest and most enthusiastic people have their doubts and begin to question if the potential rewards still justify current efforts or hardships. In these moments, self-defeat finds a comfortable home in your mind, distress takes over, and giving up seems like the best option.

I tend to feel discouraged when I don't make progress fast enough. If I don't see immediate results, however minute, my brain is quick to hit the high road and start looking for the next big thing to focus on. But my heart persuades me to think about the big picture and properly assess the situation. And, ironically, these moments of doubt often occur right at the brink of a breakthrough, or when opportunity is right around the corner, and I'm always so grateful that I didn't give up.

Your dreams put you in the driver's seat on your road to success. When you're uncertain of the direction you're going in, answer these twelve questions. Don't *just* ask yourself, reach for your tablet, laptop, or trusted pen and paper (if you're a dinosaur like me), and *answer* them. Getting your dreams out of your head and into the world, if only on a post-it, will help make the abstract nature of them more tangible and realistic.

1. **Why did I want to pursue this dream?** Dreams, unlike ideas, are more than fleeting thoughts. They follow you into your subconscious and begin to control your actions and decisions in your conscious state. They have purpose, and spark an unrivaled feeling of motivation that inspires us to commit to making them a reality. Getting to the root of why you wanted to pursue this dream in the first place often helps to determine if it's still something you want and allows you to regain enthusiasm.

2. **Did I set a REAL goal?** If you didn't identify a goal that resonates with you, empowers you, and is actionable and lucrative, it's no wonder you're considering throwing in the towel. It's difficult to keep your momentum and make something happen if you haven't tied it to the core of your being. So, stop what you're doing and set yourself a REAL goal and give yourself a real chance to succeed… pun intended.

3. **What has changed since I originally set out on my quest?** Life comes at you fast. Wants, needs, and priorities do change, and that's okay. There's no sense in committing to something that no longer serves you just to salvage the sunk cost or time spent. However, if it does still serve you, perhaps your brain, like mine, flipped a switch because your efforts have yet to yield results. If what has changed is that it has become uncomfortable, GOOD. It should be uncomfortable. Everything you want that you don't have is outside of your comfort zone.

4. **Am I afraid of failing?** What if they judge me? What if I make a mistake? What if it's a waste of time? Fear of failure

is ever-present in new journeys *if* you allow it to be. When you change your perception of fear, it can no longer control you. Setting expectations is a big part of letting fear go. If your dream is to one day open your own gym, you'll be much less afraid of failing if you set your expectations, little by little, to understand your market, how much it's going to cost, what location makes the most sense, and what the business model will look like. Fear of the unknown is usually the culprit for believing we'll fail. The more you know, the less scary it is and more possible it becomes.

5. **What's worse, not getting it right the first time, or not trying at all?** Think about why you want so badly to get it right. Now think, *so what if I get it wrong?* But really… SO WHAT? Yes, there are times when you may only have one opportunity to hit the nail on the head, but for everything else, does it *really* matter if it takes a couple of tries? Why should learning how to improve yourself prevent you from trying in the first place? Nobody is perfect. I'm not telling you anything that you don't know here. So why hold yourself to such a silly standard? Maybe you'll suck, but maybe you'll be great. Reframe your questions of self-doubt like this instead: What's better, getting it right the first time and discovering you're as awesome as you knew you could be, or learning that "right" comes in many shapes and sizes, and although it took a couple of tries you've been able to refine your skills? All of a sudden, you're faced with a win-win. This is the power of framing a question.

6. **Am I afraid of succeeding?** Fear of success can be just as debilitating as fear of failure. What will success look like? What if I have/want to move? What if it cuts into time with

my family? We often have the drive to go for our dreams, but we are afraid of what achieving them will entail. Open and honest communication with those your success will impact will help you to understand if, and how, things might change. It will also prepare you to plan for such changes and minimize the stress that comes with them.

7. **Do I have what it takes?** This is an important question to ask. Maybe you've gotten lazy, or you know you're capable, but your fire has dimmed to a small flame. Or perhaps you're lacking knowledge, funds, or support to make your dreams come true. Knowing where you're falling short and thinking about what it will take to get back on track is sometimes all you need to do to remind yourself that this dream isn't dead in the water. It just needs a little help.

8. **Who is killing my vibe?** Not everyone will be on your team and some are rooting for you to drop the ball. Figure out who they are, make sure they're not part of your inner circle of influence, and use their negativity to power your success. While I don't think you should pursue success to spite them, there's something so immensely satisfying about proving them wrong.

9. **When has there been a time that I thought I couldn't, but eventually I did?** Success isn't always butterflies and rainbows. There are many sleepless nights, moments of frustration, and risks that are taken that all go into making it possible, *but it is possible*. We're quick to lose sight of all that we're capable of in moments of doubt. Thinking of a time where you weren't sure that you'd win the battle, but then came out on top, still swinging, is a helpful exercise to

remind yourself that you're capable of more than you give yourself credit for. Remind yourself of these times often and you'll notice your library of winning moments will start to grow.

10. **Who will benefit from my pursuit of my dream?** When you answered why you're pursuing your dream, chances are you weren't thinking exclusively about yourself. Maybe you want to have your own business so you can work flexible hours and spend more quality time with your children. Or, maybe you want to find a higher paying opportunity at work so you can save for a comfortable retirement for you and your partner. Whatever your motive, think about the impact achieving your goal will have on those you care about when doing it for yourself isn't motivation enough.

11. **What advice would I give my friend if they were in my situation?** Why is it that advice comes so naturally when we're giving it to others, but when the time comes to turn it inward we drop it like a hot potato? The notion of giving advice to others but not being able to apply it to our own lives is known as the Solomon Paradox, based on a series of studies by Igor Grossman and Ethan Kross. They chose the term Solomon Paradox because of the Biblical King Solomon, known for his incredible wisdom and ability to guide others, but unable to employ that same wisdom to his own life, ultimately leading to the demise of his kingdom. See, you shouldn't be so hard on yourself: even kings struggle with this.

But the real takeaway here is that throughout their studies of this paradox, Grossman and Kross discovered that thinking about the advice that you would give to a friend hypothetically in the same situation as yourself actually helps you to make better decisions. Why? Before giving a friend advice, you're more likely to ask for further information about the circumstances of the conflict, consider other perspectives and potential outcomes, and to search for a compromise. So, before giving up, ask yourself what advice you'd give to someone in your situation and take your own advice.

12. **Am I all talk?** It's not enough to say you're going to do it, you have to actually do it. In fact, you probably shouldn't say much at all. Contrary to conventional wisdom that has taught us to share our goals with others, psychologists theorize that doing so makes you less likely to achieve them. By telling someone your goal and having them respond positively to it, the satisfaction you feel triggers the same sense of accomplishment as if your goal has been reached. This is called a "social reality," and it gets you nowhere. Success requires hard work. There will be many sacrifices; a few grey hairs may pop up—it's part of the game. Put your big boy/girl pants on and put in the time. Ask yourself if you've done everything you could to make your dream a reality. If the answer is no, keep pushing.

Bossing Up in Action

Mitchell Haynes, Pilot, Middle East

"I was not born to be a pilot, like some second and third generation pilots, I was bred to be one. My parental unit was split living in different cities. My father was in export when I was younger so he would circumnavigate the globe on a monthly basis. Many of my weekends involved packing my bag and sleeping in hotels or flying to see him. That's how I caught the bug. I always loved airplanes and in the back of my mind thought it would be nice to fly one day but it didn't seem realistic, so I prioritized other things. But the more I did other things, the more I questioned why being a pilot was unrealistic. As it turns out, there really wasn't much in my way. I got my shit together, I made some life changes and decided to try and make a career out of flying.

Every pilot has a unique story about how they ended up in the seat they are occupying and each one will tell you about how they had to pay their dues to get there. I was no different. After I graduated flight school I drove across Eastern Canada to every major airport, community airport and grass strip I could to look for work. I spent countless hours online looking for aviation companies in Canada to forward my resume to. Every spare moment was spent knocking on virtual doors, trying to get my foot in the door, but I got no responses.

At the time I was working as a baggage handler, doing whatever I could to keep myself close to an airplane. I had a few other jobs after that, all in the aviation field—though not in the pilot seat—and all were far from glamorous, but they taught me some of the best lessons of my career."

My best advice for someone trying to achieve their dream is to put your head down, shut your mouth, don't get involved in other people's misery and grind hard, really hard. Do whatever you have to do, go wherever you have to go and when you begin your career don't ever think any job is beneath you. The biggest misconception about success is that if you work hard, success will fall into your lap. It goes beyond hard work. You have to be able to see the bigger picture, leave your ego at the door and elevate those around you to their fullest potential. The road to success isn't always glorious, it can be uncomfortable, but the more you push your boundaries, the more you learn about yourself and your abilities to succeed. You've got to embrace the unknown."

Bonus Question:

Is it time to pump the breaks? There's no denying the grind of success, but that's not all there is to it. If after all the blood, sweat, and tears, there's no sense of fulfillment—there's something wrong. If you have done everything within your power to pursue your dream and are suffering as a result, it may be time to ease off the gas pedal. Your efforts should bring you happiness, and if they don't in *some* capacity, walking away may indeed be the best thing to do. As a huge fan of ABC's *Shark Tank*, I see entrepreneurs chasing their dream, investing their entire life savings, their parents' retirement fund, and remortgaging their house several times over to fund something that's clearly not working. They feel like they're in too deep and can't find their way out. Whether it's a business idea or a personal goal, if you or your family's quality of life has been severely affected in pursuit of success, or if it's making you more anxious than empowered, you should reconsider your priorities. For the record, **this is not quitting**, this is making a healthy life choice. There's no shame in putting your happiness first and making that your goal. Now it's your turn, say it slow and with purpose: There—is—no—shame—in—putting—my—happiness—first—and—making—that—my—goal.

"There are some people who live in a dream world, and there are some who face reality; and then there are those who turn one into the other." - Douglas Everet

Notes

Notes

Chapter 28
There Is No Finish Line

Chuck Norris Says So, So It Must Be True

This is arguably one of the best and hardest things to accept. Many of us are obsessed with being successful and crossing the finish line to the arrival of our dreams and goals. We become so preoccupied with the end goal that we may lose sight of what we're doing it for. Without that vision, when you "get there," wherever or whatever that is for you, you may be disillusioned and unnecessarily hard on yourself. Don't give in to old habits and open the door to negativity just because success may not look or feel like you thought it would.

We're all familiar with vicious cycles. You know, when you tell yourself summer is coming up and you've got to get beach-ready so you go on a cleanse. But wait, you forgot Sarah's birthday is this Friday, so okay, that'll be a little cheat day. Thursday night rolls around and you're watching Netflix and craving chips and you cave, but tomorrow's a cheat day anyway so you'll just bundle it all together. That's how cheat days go, right? Friday's little cheat turns into a big cheat, and come Saturday you've totally fallen off the wagon, because what's the point of caring anymore? Sound familiar? You're in a vicious cycle and it started with one decision.

A "virtuous cycle" is a term that's less popular in everyday life, but is commonly used in business theory and economics, and is pretty rad. It refers to a chain of actions or events that reinforce themselves through a constant feedback loop, repeating and reinforcing positive outcomes. For example, a hotel that makes an effort to improve the quality of their service can theoretically expect better reviews and higher customer ratings that will result in additional bookings at higher rates. The resulting influx in revenue allows the hotel to continue to improve in quality, and the cycle continues.

As we know, business growth and personal growth aren't worlds apart. So, how can we apply this fancy theory to our lives and ensure a constant feedback loop of success? Simple: it starts with one decision. Consciously make that choice every day and force yourself to do something positive that you know you can do. This starts the virtuous cycle. When you do it, you'll feel good. When you feel good, you'll want to do more of it. When you do more of it, you'll start to feel even better. And just like that, you've created a positive feedback loop.

Don't let a single day go by without doing something positive that keeps the loop going and feeds into your success. If, at the end of the day, you feel like you got nothing accomplished, take one small action to remind yourself that you're in control. Do one squat, send one email, read one of the articles you bookmarked (don't give me the "I'm too tired" bullshit, you were going to check Facebook, anyway). Master the micro moments and use your time to get you ahead.

Knowing how to create and maintain a virtuous cycle of improvement is critical to success, because there really is no end to Bossing Up: opportunity and happiness aren't finite, but you need to work for them. This way of life is a constant work in progress and you must accept that every finish line is the beginning of a new race. The goal is to keep growing, creating, and overcoming obstacles. The flame that ignites your passion, dedication, and hunger for more mustn't go out. Life may dim it at times and that's okay; just keep it burning.

It can be easy to forget that behind every billion-dollar company and every entrepreneurial success story is someone who just kept going. Think about Elon Musk and Sara Blakely—they don't stop once they cross the finish line. They take a water break, start the next race, and continue to revolutionize products and services for the rest of us (yes, Spanx and SpaceX are of equal wowness in my book).

While you're running the race, remember to stay in your own lane and focus on your own progress. In Oprah's Master Class series, she shared, "Don't worry about the other guys because you cannot control them. You only have control over yourself. The energy that it takes to look back and see where the other guys are takes energy away from you and if they're too close, it scares you. Don't waste your time looking back." Your journey isn't about them anyway, it's about *you* and running that race to the best of your ability.

By embracing that there's no finish line, I'm not suggesting that you work yourself into the ground, or that your goal should be to reduce the risk of human extinction in order to be successful (though kudos to you, Elon, if you're reading this). Instead, the sentiment behind "there is no finish line" is based on the philosophy of *becoming versus getting*. When you're focused solely on what you're *getting* out of accomplishing your goals, crossing the finish line becomes your main priority. Whereas, when you're focused on what you're *becoming* in the process, as you can imagine, your priority expands beyond the goal at hand and evolves into something bigger, something that propels you across the finish line and into the next race.

"The person you become in pursuit of success is infinitely more important than anything you might get." – Samantha Kris

Welcome to the Bossing Up Family.

Notes

Extra Tips for Those Who Are Bossing Up

Fifty Random Thoughts, Instagram Posts, and Other Advice That Has Helped Me on My Bossing Up Journey

1. Note to self: you good, you poppin.
2. Relax. Everything will be okay.
3. There's no one path to success. You may get lost, you may take the scenic route, but as long as you keep moving, you'll get there.
4. There's always a solution. Realize that if you can instantly create a problem, you can just as quickly and easily create a solution.
5. People will get jealous. Remember that a flower doesn't compete with the flower next to it. It just blooms.
6. Don't be an asshole. People respond better to kindness than threats.
7. Trade your expectations for appreciation. This way, you'll never be disappointed.
8. Take a step back. It's okay to take a few steps back in order to go forward. Imagine jumping across a creek. You need to go backwards in order to gain the momentum needed to make the leap.
9. Leave your ego at the door. It's never invited to the party.
10. Happiness and success are a process. All good things are.
11. Gratitude is the antidote to fear and anger. It's hard to be afraid and angry when you're grateful.

12. Problems shared are problems halved. Let people help you carry the weight of the world; your shoulders aren't strong enough.

13. Don't wait until you've reached your goal to be proud of yourself. Be proud and celebrate every step you take.

14. There are no problems. There are only possibilities.

15. You are the CEO of your own life. You've got to evaluate the people that are in it and promote, demote, and terminate accordingly.

16. All success is created on the inside. Proceed as if success is inevitable.

17. The scariest moment is always just before you start. Take the leap. The rest is fun.

18. When life gives you more than you can stand, kneel.

19. You aren't responsible for fixing everything that's broken.

20. If it excites you and scares you at the same time, it's probably worth trying.

21. Self-destruction is not an option. Let every choice you make be a brick on your path to success.

22. Remember what's within your power to change: your attitude, your mindset, and your energy.

23. Don't focus on finding passion. Focus on being a passionate person.

24. Stop playing small. Give yourself permission to live a big life; you were meant for greater things.

25. 'No' is not the end of the road. It just means *next opportunity*.

26. You can't change your past. You can change your future.

27. Be patient.

28. If you want the rainbow, you've got to put up with the rain.

29. Start where you are and with what you have today.

30. Your thoughts dictate your actions. Think positive.

31. Be patient. Success does not come overnight, even for the "overnight success" stories.

32. If you could believe in Santa Claus for like eight years, you can believe in yourself for five seconds, okay? You got this.

33. You gotta show up.

34. Be sure to taste your words before you spit them out.

35. Strong people rarely have an easy past.

36. Remember, you're so much stronger than you think.

37. Well done is always better than well said.

38. You can only find your limits by pushing them.

39. There's enough success to go around. I promise.

40. Sometimes you just gotta let shit go. Whatever happened, happened. Stop stressing over it. You're still young and you still got more shit coming your way.

41. Intuition does not lie.

42. Do what gives you peace.

43. It's important to find comfort in your own company.

44. A lot of what weighs you down isn't yours to carry. Let it go.

45. Fear is too expensive.

46. If you're tired of starting over, stop quitting.

47. There's no traffic when you go the extra mile.

48. Happiness is an inside job.

49. Not everything works every single time. Keep trying.

50. You can. End of story.

Notes

The Bossing Up Manifesto

I promise to not sabotage my dreams before I even begin. I will believe in myself and accept that there will be moments when I might not, but those thoughts will not consume me. I will love myself, even on the days I don't feel like it. I will listen to others, take what serves me and let go of what doesn't. I will listen to the person who knows me best by listening inward. I will be open to embracing opportunity and creating it when it does not seem apparent. I will help others when it's needed and accept help when I need it; and I will need it. I will live authentically, even when I'm challenged to conform. I will accept that things change and I, too, will change with them. I will eliminate negativity from my life and refuse to settle. I will stop waiting; the time is now. I will be kind to myself when I make mistakes. I will fall, but I will rise. I will put myself first and not feel guilty. I will do everything in my power to be a good person; nobody respects an asshole. I will set goals that inspire me to take action. I will make progress every single day, however small or large. I will make it until I make it, and then I will keep going. I AM A BOSS.

Thank you

Thank You

To my parents, who have always supported me and encouraged my every idea. Your unconditional love, patience, and perseverance have made me unstoppable. Thanks especially to my mom, who's been my strength when I've had none. To Siobhan, Alex, Melyssa, and Jamie, being your sister has been my greatest joy and most honored title. You have inspired me through the darkest of days, you will never know how much I love you and how grateful I am that life has brought us together. To my friends who have been there through tears of laughter and sorrow, your friendship will forever be treasured. To my clients who allow me to live my dream every day. To the Bosses who contributed their stories, and to all those I've met and have yet to meet, your encouragement and dedication to the Bossing Up movement inspire me to take action every day. To Graham, who has been my biggest cheerleader and has kept me accountable and excited about my goals. And to you, the reader—thank you.

No thanks to my upstairs neighbor who seems to use his hallway as a bowling alley and his living room as a jungle gym—with no regard for time or volume levels. You, sir, are an asshole.

A Peek Behind the Curtain of My Procrastinating Mind

Things I Catch Myself Thinking When I Should Be Focused on Writing

April 20, 2016 - 5:55 PM – I just got off the phone with a publishing company and I think I've got a real shot at this author thing. Not because they suckered me into thinking I'm going to be the next *New York Times* bestseller, but because, as I explained the concept of the book, I felt like it was something I would read. I genuinely feel like it's going to be useful for anyone looking to elevate their inner boss.

May 9, 2016 - 2:19 PM – One of my life goals was to write my first book before I turn thirty.

If I start now, it's totally doable. I have thirteen months. I've got this.

May 28, 2016 - 10:43 PM – I still have not started.

June 19, 2016 - 5:02 PM – I still have not started. Adulting is hard.

July 27, 2016 - 6:12 AM – Today I'm twenty-nine. You guessed it… I still have not started. What the fuck is wrong with me? JUST START ALREADY. The twelve-month countdown is on.

August 3, 2016 - 7:34 AM – I figured out why I've been dragging my ass. I haven't set a REAL goal yet. You'd think I'd have this figured out by now. Okay, time to get real (pun unintended).

August 5, 2016 - 11:11 PM – Writing has officially started and it's off to a good start. I deserve ~~a break~~ to keep going. Type, monkey, type!

August 22, 2016 - 8:18 PM – Why do mothers only get a day when sharks get a whole week? This is a cruel and unfair world we live in.

September 4, 2016 - 12: 36 AM – Writing is going well, but my brain is totally fried. One final thought for the night, though I guess it's morning now: literally every choice I've ever made has led me to writing this exact sentence; and every choice you've ever made has led you to reading it… that's deep.

September 13, 2016 - 3:39 PM – Some of us are still "it" from our childhood game of tag.

September 15, 2016 - 5:15 PM – Today I decided I'm "unfuckwithable." Nothing dramatic happened, no one tried to do me wrong, but it just so perfectly encapsulates today's vibe. I'm at peace with myself. Nothing anyone says or does can bother me and no negativity can touch me. I've got to figure out a way to bottle this up and sell it; this is the good shit.

September 22, 2016 - 5:26 PM – I legitimately have about twenty-five names for each of my dogs. All of them have been made into their own song. All of them are tested by the Batman theme song. If they sound good after "nananananananana," they make the cut and last at least 2 months.

October 9, 2016 - 11:10 AM – WTF was I thinking writing a book!? I couldn't have picked an easier life goal, like… learning how to speak Spanish fluently? I know "dónde está el baño" and "que hora es"… I'm already halfway there. Sheesh.

November 1, 2016 - 9:00 PM – I read a *Huffington Post* article this morning that says we have between 50,000 – 70,000 thoughts per day, which means between thirty-five and forty-eight thoughts per minute. I'm thinking about this book and what to write about around the clock... assuming I could articulate a thought in about ten words, I just need to scribe two minutes' worth of thoughts per day to meet my daily word count goal. That's how this whole writing thing works, right?

November 23, 2016 - 8:47 PM – Folding fitted sheets is literally THE WORST.

December 1, 2016 - 4:12 PM – It was so hard saying no to a contract today. The man was super nice, the project seemed interesting, and the money was good, but it didn't feel right. I know that he would've taken every ounce of my energy and would never have been satisfied. Not all business is good business... that's still not an easy one to accept.

December 7, 2016 - 12:30 AM – I hosted an incredible workshop tonight. I'm on cloud nine.

December 11, 2016 - 1:04 PM – I just saw a Smucker's ad online (yeah, the jam company). Not only was I surprised to see they have over 150 products, I'm baffled by the idea of buying jam online, but now I'm curious. Well played, Smucker's.

December 31, 2016 - 3:09 PM – I don't care much for New Year's resolutions and setting goals just because it's a "fresh start." Setting goals is something I do regularly, but I do like cracking open a new agenda and filling it with notes... these notes just happen to be goal-related on New Year's Eve. Among 2017's goals are: travel somewhere new for pleasure instead of work, secure a TV appearance, and finish Bossing Up.

January 8, 2017 - 3:17 PM – I wish I could take back all those times I didn't want to nap when I was younger. *Forehead hits the keyboard*

January 31, 2017 - 4:12 PM – Why is it that when I'm in traffic, out for lunch, or on a call, I have a million and one things I want to write about; yet the minute I sit in front of my computer I draw a blank?

February 6, 2017 - 11:05 AM – There are sirens blaring, car horns honking, and people screaming outside. It legit sounds like the zombie apocalypse is starting, but I guess I'll have to find out the hard way because I. Must. Reach. Today's. Writing. Goal.

February 13, 2017 - 7:43 AM – I didn't reach yesterday's writing goal, but I wrote my heart out and made some great headway today. Remember: progress - not perfection (takes deep, calming breath).

February 15, 2017 - 6:16 PM – I just bought tickets to go see Chance The Rapper and got a ticket to a woman's networking event for the same night. I will be showing up to the rap concert dressed like a yuppie. I'm a complex individual.

March 5, 2017 - 9:27 PM – It's the day after a major snowfall, which makes me just want to curl up and sleep. Instead, today was a full day of back-to-back meetings. I didn't even have time to pee... who doesn't make time to PEE?! Crazy people, THAT'S WHO. By the time I got in, walked the dogs, made dinner (which was a bowl of cereal), gave one of the dogs a bath, did the dishes, and Skyped with a client, I decided I was done with today. I promised myself I would write, though. So, here I am, writing... albeit completely useless stuff, but I didn't specify what I had to write. Aha, a loophole! This will count if it makes it into the book, right? Note to self: use that bit about pee somewhere in the book... I can't be the only one who sacrifices their bladder for a strike of creative genius.

March 12, 2017 - 9:12 PM – The clocks 'sprung forward' today, which means spring is around the corner and it will be summer before we know it and this will have evolved into a LEGIT book... with actual pages and a cover. I cannot wait to crack open the spine of MY OWN book. Shit is getting real, y'all!

March 23, 2017 - 2:32 AM – Add just covered voice typing. And it's pretty sitting. Translated: *I just discovered voice typing, and it's pretty shitty.*

March 30, 2017 - 8:26 PM – I read in a *Psychology Today* article that 46 percent of Americans are afraid of the deep end of a pool.

April 5, 2017 - 11:04 AM – I wonder what dogs dream about?

April 21, 2017 - 5:38 PM – Sat down to write, gave myself a manicure instead. You win some, you lose some.

April 29, 2017 - 8:09 PM – I searched urban dictionary for 'bossing up', which lead to 'big up yourself' and I got this as a definition: *Praise yourself; big up yerself rude bwoi.* I wish I hadn't told so many people the name of this book... I would've totally gone with that definition as the title.

May 2, 2017 - 8:17 PM – Dutch, my jack russell, felt compelled to contribute his literary genius to this project. With his head and paws, he wants to share:

'++
999..9966663'

May 8, 2017 - 12:18 PM – I'm sick. On the down side: having a cold really blows. I'm bundled up in a wool sweater drinking Neocitran out of a tin cup like a modern cavewoman. On the up side: Neocitran is delicious. I don't care what anyone says.

May 25, 2017 - 3:33 AM – I keep having dreams that I'm out with no bra. I wonder what that means.

May 25, 2017 - 8:01 AM – Apparently no-bra dreams are a sign of feeling rebellious. I'm totally wearing my leather pants today.

May 29, 2017 - 4:30 AM – I have my TV debut today on Global News. REAL goals for the win! I'm SO ready to share my message and get Bossing Up on the map. This deserves a celebration… fuck it, I'm buying the shoes!

June 4, 2017 - 5:57 PM – Have you ever wondered why you yawn more when you're cold? Apparently, it's your body's way of keeping your brain cool, and like your computer, it performs better when it's not overheated. The more you know.

June 7, 2017 - 6:32 AM – Real talk, guys – the amount of changes that were made to my first draft of this book were pretty discouraging. I didn't expect to hit the nail on the head the first time around, nor did I expect it to be easy, but God damn… keeping my head up to get this over the finish line is taking all the strength I've got. It will be worth it.

A Peek Behind the Curtain of My Procrastinating Mind

June 16, 2017 - 12:04 AM – The book goes into editorial today. It will officially be out of my hands and getting prepped for the world. What a fucking scary and exciting feeling. This has been the most vulnerable I've ever felt. I trust that I'm in good hands. Thank you Bosses!

Bibliography

Anderson, Kare. "Be an Opportunity Maker." Filmed September 2014. TED video, 9:46. Posted November 2014. https://www.ted.com/talks/kare_anderson_be_an_opportunity_maker.

Bellinger, D. B., B. M. Budde, M. Machida, G. B. Richardson, and W. P. Berg. 2009. "The effect of cellular telephone conversation and music listening on response time in braking." Transportation Research Part F: Traffic Psychology and Behaviour 12 (6), 441-451.

Cabrera, Marquis. 2014. "Use Co-opetition to Build New Lines of Revenue." hbr.org. Published February 10. https://hbr.org/2014/02/use-co-opetition-to-build-new-lines-of-revenue.

"Cognitive therapy." 2017. Wikipedia. Published June 16. https://en.wikipedia.org/wiki/Cognitive_therapy.

Cuddy, Amy. "Your Body Language May Shape Who You Are." Filmed June 2012. TED video, 21:02. Posted October 2012. https://www.ted.com/talks/amy_cuddy_your_body_language_shapes_who_you_are?language=en.

Dachis, Adam. 2013. "How to Choose Your Battles and Fight for What Actually Matters." lifehacker.com. Published March 11.

http://lifehacker.com/5989295/how-to-choose-your-battles-and-fight-for-what-actually-   matters.

Effron, Lauren. 2016. "Michael Jordan, Kobe Bryant's Meditation Coach on How to Be 'Flow Ready' and Get in the Zone." abcnews.go.com. Published April 6. http://abcnews.go.com/Health/michael-jordan-kobe-bryants-meditation-coach-flow-ready/story?id=38175801.

"Emotional Intelligence." MindTools. Accessed May, 2017. https://www.mindtools.com/pages/article/newCDV_59.htm

Fernandez, Alvaro. 2008. "Why Do You Turn Down the Radio When You're Lost?" huffingtonpost.com. Published February 26. http://www.huffingtonpost.com/alvaro-fernandez/why-do-you-turn-down-the-_b_88629.html.

Flynn, Francis. "What Makes People Want to Help Others?" Stanford Graduate School of Business. Accessed February, 2017 https://www.gsb.stanford.edu/insights/francis-flynn-what-makes-people-want-help-others

Freaks, Data. 2015. "Why We Give Great Advice To Others But Can't Take it Ourselves." forbes.com. Published April 7. https://www.forbes.com/forbes/welcome/?toURL=https://www.forbes.com/sites/datafreaks/2015/04/07/why-we-give-great-advice-to-others-but-cant-take-it-ourselves/&refURL=&referrer=#5ea0850c1515.

Garner, Janine. 2015. From Me to We: Why Commercial Collaboration Will Future-proof Business, Leaders and Personal Success. Melbourne: Wrightbooks.

Gilbertson, Tina. 2014. "Fear of Failure?" psychologytoday.com. Published May 12.

https://www.psychologytoday.com/blog/constructive-wallowing/201405/fear-failure.

Gorlick, Adam. 2009. "Media multitaskers pay mental price, Stanford study shows." news.stanford.edu. Published August 24. http://news.stanford.edu/2009/08/24/multitask-research-study-082409/.

Hallowell, E. M. 2005. "Overloaded circuits: Why smart people underperform." Harvard Business Review, January 1.

Harrold, Ed. 2014. "A Breathing Exercise To Help You Live in The Moment." Mindbodygreen.com. Published July 16. https://www.mindbodygreen.com/0-14524/a-breathing-exercise-to-help-you-live-in-the-moment.html.

"How To Retain 90% Of Everything You Learn." 2015. Psychotactics. Published August 13. https://www.psychotactics.com/art-retain-learning/.

"How to Win Friends and Influence People." 2017. Wikipedia. Published June 20.

https://en.wikipedia.org/wiki/How_to_Win_Friends_and_Influence_People.

Hyman, Gary. "How To Find Your Unique Selling Proposition by Authentic Personal Branding." Social Media Strategies Techniques For Business Professionals. Accessed March, 2017.
http://www.garyhyman.com/how-to-find-your-unique-selling-proposition-by-authentic-personal-branding/

Gregory, Alyssa. "7 Steps for Writing a Powerful Elevator Pitch." The Balance. Updated June, 2017.

https://www.thebalance.com/how-to-write-an-elevator-pitch-2951690

"Identifying negative thinking." 2017. Mayo Clinic. Published February 18.
http://www.mayoclinic.org/healthy-lifestyle/stress-management/in-depth/positive-thinking/art-20043950?pg=2.

Jussiecatwriter. 2014. "The Importance of Authenticity." selfavenue.com. Accessed March 2017.
http://selfavenue.com/the-importance-of-authenticity/.

Just, Marcel Adam, Timothy A. Keller, and Jacquelyn Cynkar. 2008. "A Decrease in Brain Activation Associated with Driving When Listening to Someone Speak."ncbi.nlm.nih.gov. Published April 18.
https://www.ncbi.nlm.nih.gov/pmc/articles/PMC2713933/.

Kane, Becky. 2015. "The Science of Analysis Paralysis: How Overthinking Kills Your Productivity & What You Can Do About It." Todoist Blog. Published July 8.
https://blog.todoist.com/2015/07/08/analysis-paralysis-and-your-productivity/.

Khrapov, Alex. 2014. "Why I Never Use "life balance wheel" Tool In My Coaching Practice." linkedin.com. Published June 21.
https://www.linkedin.com/pulse/20140621112736-23732165-why-i-never-use-life-balance-wheel-tool-in-my-coaching-practice.

Kim, Brian. "Why It's Important to Be Authentic." briankim.net. Accessed April, 2017.
http://briankim.net/articles/important-authentic/.

Bibliography

McLeod, Saul. 2008. "Cognitive Dissonance." simplypsychology.org. Accessed April, 2017. https://www.simplypsychology.org/cognitive-dissonance.html.

Napier, Nancy K. 2014. "The Myth of Multitasking." psychologytoday.com. Published May 12. https://www.psychologytoday.com/blog/creativity-without-borders/201405/the-myth- multitasking.

Oragui, David. 2016. "The Balanced Wheel of Life." balancedlifeacademy.com. Published February 14. https://balancedlifeacademy.com/balanced-wheel-of-life/.

Peters, Tom. 1997. "The Brand Called You." Fast Company. Published May 18, 2017. https://www.fastcompany.com/28905/brand-called-you

Ritala, Paavo, Arash Golnam, and Alain Wegmann. 2014. "Coopetition-based business models: The case of Amazon.com." Industrial Marketing Management 43 (2): 236-249. http://www.sciencedirect.com/science/article/pii/S0019850113002150.

Sivers, Derek. "Keep Your Goals to Yourself." Filmed July 2010. TED video, 3:15. Posted September 2010. https://www.ted.com/talks/derek_sivers_keep_your_goals_to_yourself.

Stavros, Jacqueline M. 2009. The Thin Book of Soar: Building Strengths-Based Strategy. Bend: Thin Book Publishing Co.

Sundem, Garth. 2012. "This Is Your Brain on Multitasking." psychologytoday.com. Published February 24.

https://www.psychologytoday.com/blog/brain-trust/201202/is-your-brain- multitasking.

Tavris, Carol, and Elliot Aronson. 2008. Mistakes Were Made (But Not by Me): Why We Justify Foolish Beliefs, Bad Decisions, and Hurtful Acts. Boston: Houghton Mifflon Harcourt Publishing Company.

Underwood, B.J., and L. Postman. 1960. "Extra-experimental sources of interference in forgetting." Psychological Review 67, 73-95.

"Virtuous circle and vicious circle." 2017. Wikipedia. Published July 9. https://en.wikipedia.org/wiki/Virtuous_circle_and_vicious_circle.

Winch, Guy. 2013. "10 Signs That You Might Have Fear of Failure." psychologytoday.com. Published June 18. https://www.psychologytoday.com/blog/the-squeaky-wheel/201306/10-signs-you-might-have-fear-failure.

Wojcicki, Susan. 2011. "The Eight Pillars of Innovation." thinkwithgoogle.com. Published July. https://www.thinkwithgoogle.com/marketing-resources/8-pillars-of-innovation/.

"2014 MUM Graduation Jim Carrey." YouTube video, 7:42. Posted by "Maharishi University of Management," May 27, 2014. https://www.youtube.com/watch?v=4AOQgrNKLWM.

Links

Become a member of the Bossing Up family by joining the Facebook group: www.facebook.com/groups/BossingUp/

For more Bossing Up tips and tools, check out Samantha's blog: http://www.samanthakris.com/bossing-up-blog/

Never miss a beat by signing up to the Bossing Up newsletter: http://www.samanthakris.com/contact/

Learn more about Samantha at www.samanthakris.com

www.ingramcontent.com/pod-product-compliance
Lightning Source LLC
Chambersburg PA
CBHW020036120526
44589CB00032B/389